TOP SECRET FILES

The Wild West

TOP SECRET FILES

The **Wild West**

STEPHANIE BEARCE

PRUFROCK PRESS INC.
WACO, TEXAS

Library of Congress Cataloging-in-Publication Data

Bearce, Stephanie, author.
Top secret files : the wild west / by Stephanie Bearce.
    1 online resource.
Description based on print version record and CIP data provided by publisher; resource
not viewed.
ISBN 978-1-61821-462-1 (Paperback)
ISBN 978-1-61821-463-8 (PDF)
ISBN 978-1-61821-512-3 (ePub)
1. West (U.S.)--History--Juvenile literature. 2. Frontier and pioneer life--West (U.S.)--
Juvenile literature. I. Title. II. Title: Wild west.
F591
978--dc23
                        2015032979

Copyright ©2016 Prufrock Press Inc.

Edited by Lacy Compton

Cover and layout design by Raquel Trevino

ISBN-13: 978-1-61821-462-1

Printed in the United States of America.

At the time of this book's publication, all facts and figures cited are the most current
available. All telephone numbers, addresses, and website URLs are accurate and active.
All publications, organizations, websites, and other resources exist as described in the
book, and all have been verified. The author and Prufrock Press Inc. make no warranty
or guarantee concerning the information and materials given out by organizations or
content found at websites, and we are not responsible for any changes that occur after
this book's publication. If you find an error, please contact Prufrock Press Inc.

Prufrock Press Inc.
P.O. Box 8813
Waco, TX 76714-8813
Phone: (800) 998-2208
Fax: (800) 240-0333
http://www.prufrock.com

TABLE OF CONTENTS

WESTWARD HO!

LEGENDS AND LORE

COWBOYS AND COWGIRLS

LAWMEN AND OUTLAWS

VAQUEROS TO COWBOYS

Imagine looking out across the Texas prairie and seeing hundreds of longhorn cattle roaming the plains—all free for the taking. Hundreds, thousands of cattle just wandering the grasslands, getting nice and fat on nutritious green grass. If a person could figure out how to round them up and get them to market, they would be worth a fortune.

Spanish settlers brought thousands of head of cattle to New Mexico in 1598. The cattle roamed the open range and because there were no fences, some of the cattle eventually wandered off from the larger herds. Over the next 400 years, the cows had calves and the numbers of wild cattle increased into the thousands.

Vaqueros were hired by wealthy Mexican caballeros (gentlemen) to round up the cattle and herd them hundreds of miles from the ranges of Texas and New Mexico to the market in Mexico City.

The vaqueros had to be skilled horsemen. They knew how to ride fast to race down a wandering steer. They swung braided rope lariats in the air and caught wandering cattle in their noose. With their wide-brimmed sombreros, leather chaps, and jangling spurs, to be a vaquero was a respected profession. It required skill and training. It also required physical strength and agility, brains, and common sense.

In 1821, the first Anglo settlers arrived in Texas. It must have seemed like winning the lottery to these people—they came to settle the land and found it populated with thousands of cattle free for the taking. The English-speaking men quickly learned from the vaqueros. Some of the Texas ranchers hired the vaqueros to help round up cattle. The Texans called their cattle handlers *cowboys*. They wore the same wide sombreros and leather chaps. They learned to rope, tie, and wrestle the cattle just like the vaqueros.

By the time the Civil War started in 1861, there was a flourishing cattle trade supplying meat to other parts of the United States. But just as the Civil War tore the country apart, it also hurt the cattle ranches. Cowboys rode off to join the war and the cattle roamed untended for the next 4 years.

At the end of the Civil War, the Texas cowboys and ranchers came home to find their prairies once again overpopulated with longhorn cattle. Cattle in Texas sold for only $2 per head. But in the eastern and northern United States there was a shortage of meat. In the North, one cow was worth $30!

Ranchers hired cowboys to round up the cattle and drive them north from Texas to the railroad towns in Kansas. They put the cattle in livestock cars and shipped them to the meat-hungry people in New York, Connecticut, Massachusetts, and other Eastern states. Even with the cost of paying the cowboys and railcars, the ranchers still made huge profits. From 1865 through the 1880s, more than 10 million cattle were herded by cowboys to the Kansas rails. It was the same thing the Vaqueros had done years before, except the cattle were driven north instead of south.

One of the most popular routes was the Chisholm Trail that went from San Antonio, TX, to Abilene, KS. Other rail towns were Ellsworth, Junction City, Newton, and Wichita, KS. Other routes like the Goodnight-Loving Trail ended in Colorado, where ranchers sold cattle to miners and the military.

A typical cattle drive had 3,000 head of cattle and was managed by 11 cowboys. Most of the cowboys were between the ages of 12 and 18. These teenagers learned the skills of herding and roping on the job and were paid about $30 a month.

Trail bosses were cowboys who had experience, but they were also young men. Most of them were just in their twenties. Trail bosses had to manage all of the younger cowboys, or "waddies" as the trail bosses called them. Trail bosses were also expected to locate water and good grass for the cattle on the trail, handle the money, purchase supplies, pay tolls, and keep an eye out for predators. A trail boss was often paid $100 a month. The average worker earned $15 per month in 1866. Cooks were almost as important as the trail bosses. They earned $75 per month for keeping the cowboys riding on a full stomach.

Riding the trail was sometimes just plain boring. The cattle walked in a line munching grass as they walked. The cowboys didn't hurry them, because the more they ate, the more weight they gained and cattle were sold by the pound. Most cattle gained weight eating their way to market. It could take anywhere from 25 to 100 days to herd the cattle to town.

The idea of cowboys galloping along shooting guns is actually just a myth shown in movies and on television. The young cowboys were not allowed to carry guns while they were on the trail. Firearms were kept under the watchful eye of the cook and stored in the chuck wagon. The trail boss carried a gun to protect the cattle against wild animals and very rarely to warn off rustlers.

Once the cowboys reached the rail yards and the cattle were loaded, they received their pay. The temptation to spend their money in town was huge. There were saloons, gambling, and pretty girls to squander their money on. Smart cowboys saved most of their pay. They knew they wouldn't get paid again until they had ridden home and then done another trail ride. It was a seasonal job because they couldn't move the cattle in bad weather. Many young cowboys finished the trail ride and went back home to work on the family farm or attend school. For some, it was the adventure of a lifetime. For others, it was the start of their career as a cowboy.

The Calf Sack

Rancher Charles Goodnight had a special wagon built to carry any calves that were born along the trail. Because the calves could not keep up with the adult animals, they rode in the wagon during the day. At night, they stayed with their mothers. Problem was, a mother cow knows her calf by its smell, so with several calves on the wagon the smells got mixed up and the mothers wouldn't nurse them.

Goodnight solved this problem by having the cowboys place each calf in a numbered sack each morning. At night, they were taken out of the sack and stayed with their mothers. This method worked. The calves kept their individual scents and the cows nursed their calves.

CHUCK WAGON CHARLIE

Charles Goodnight is given the credit for inventing the chuck wagon. Before the chuck wagon came into use, cowboys had to eat what they could carry in their saddlebags, which was not delicious food. They ate dried beef or hard biscuits. They softened the biscuits by dunking them in water. If they were lucky, they might shoot a rabbit or squirrel and be able to cook some fresh meat, but that was rare. Cowboys out on the range spent a lot of time with growling stomachs.

Goodnight knew that a hungry cowboy was not able to work as hard as a cowboy who had eaten a good meal. He took a surplus Army wagon and added a big pantry box to the back. The box had a hinged door that could be laid flat to create a smooth work surface. There were shelves and drawers inside the pantry to hold pots and pans and cooking gear. The wagon became so popular that Studebaker began selling its own line of chuck wagons called the "Round-Up."

Cowboys seated around chuckwagon at campsite, 1887

The chuck in chuck wagon was not actually for Charles Goodnight. It was a slang word that meant good, hearty food. And to the cowboys, it was much better food than dried beef and biscuits.

The menu almost always included beans and a strong cup of coffee. Beef was always available and sometimes they would have fresh eggs and vegetables. It was the job of the trail boss to trade with local farmers along the way for fresh cooking supplies.

Cowboys literally licked their plates clean. This helped out the cook so his clean-up job was easier. Once the plate had been thoroughly licked, it was placed in a tub of water and the cook cleaned up.

As soon as breakfast was finished, the cook would pack up the wagon and head out on the trail. It was the cook's job to find the place to camp for the night. He set up ahead of the slow-moving cattle and cowboys and had a meal waiting when the cowboys arrived in the evening.

Beef stew was one of the most common dinners, and chili was another dish that was popular. If the cook was in a good mood and he had the right ingredients, he might make a peach cobbler or an apple pie. The smell of the chuck wagon supper cooking helped many cowboys make it through the day.

Test out your chuck wagon cooking skills with this recipe.

SCALLOPED CORN

Ingredients

- ❑ 2 cups corn
- ❑ 2/3 cup milk
- ❑ 1 1/4 tsp. salt
- ❑ Dash of pepper
- ❑ 1 slightly beaten egg
- ❑ 2 tbsp. butter or margarine, melted
- ❑ 2 cups soft bread crumbs

Mix corn, egg, milk, and seasonings. Mix crumbs and butter and place 1/4 of mixture in bottom of buttered dish. Add half of the corn mixture, then another 1/4 of crumbs. Repeat layers, ending with the balance of crumbs. Bake 30 minutes at 350 degrees. Serve hot and enjoy!

For more chuck wagon recipes, see page 24

COWBOY CODE

Three cowboys taking a break against a wooden fence, 1940

Cowboys followed a special code of conduct. The rules weren't written down in a handbook or printed on paper, but every cowboy knew the rules. Breaking the rules meant becoming the butt of jokes or even getting a fist in the face.

Some of the rules were just plain common sense. For example, never wave at a man who is riding a horse. If you wave, there is a chance you will spook his horse and cause it to rear up. If the cowboy falls off, he is not going to be happy you waved at him. Instead, you should nod to a cowboy on a horse.

Other rules were about courtesy and attitude. Cowboys were allowed to cuss, but only around men, horses, and cows. It was considered very rude to cuss around women or children. Cowboys were expected to have a good attitude. Complaining was for quitters and cowboys hated quitters.

Then there were rules that actually were laws, like never steal another man's horse. It was against the law to steal anything in the West, but stealing a man's horse was one of the worst crimes a person could commit. The West was a large place and there weren't very many sheriffs or police available, so if you were caught stealing a man's horse you understood that you might get hung without a trial.

And some of the rules were funny sayings, but they always had some deeper truth to them. For example, cowboys warned young waddies (new boys) to always drink water upstream from the herd. Nobody wanted to accidentally be drinking in a stream where the cattle had just peed. But it also meant that you should be aware of what is going on around you and not make stupid mistakes that could be prevented.

HERE ARE SOME OF THE RULES OF THE COWBOY CODE:

* Never shoot an unarmed man.
* Never shoot a woman at all.
* Never try on another cowboy's hat.
* Remove your guns before sitting at the dining table.
* Never try to wake up a cowboy by shaking him. He just might roll over and shoot you.

❋ Honesty is a cowboy's most valuable asset. Your word is your bond and a handshake is more binding than a contract written by some fancy lawyer.

❋ Don't squat with your spurs on. It hurts.

❋ Never miss a good chance to shut up. Cowboys don't talk too much. They save their breath for breathing. They only talk when it really matters.

❋ When approaching somebody from the back, always yell out a big howdy before you get within shooting range.

❋ When you get to the chuck wagon, don't sit around waiting for everyone else to show up. Get your food, eat it, and make way for the next cowboy.

❋ Respect the land. Take care of the trees, grass, and keep the water clean. Don't light fires where there is dry timber.

❋ The fastest way to double your money is to fold it over and put it back in your pocket. (Save your money!)

❋ Never pass anyone on the trail without saying howdy.

❋ After you pass someone on the trail, never look back at him. It implies you don't trust him.

❋ Never approach a bull from the front, a horse from the rear, or a fool from any direction.

❋ Live a good, honorable life. Then when you get old and think back, you'll enjoy it a second time.

~ FUN FACT ~
ROY ROGERS' RULES

Many Happy Trails to you always. Sincerely, Roy Rogers

Roy Rogers and his reliable horse, Trigger, 1938

During the 1950s and 1960s, children in America loved watching cowboy shows on television and in the movies. Some of the popular shows were *The Lone Ranger*, *Bonanza*, *The Big Valley*, *The Roy Rogers Show*, and *Gunsmoke*. Almost every night, kids could turn on the television to watch cowboys herding cattle and fighting bad guys. The shows were so popular that some of the movie stars wrote out their own set of cowboy rules to help kids learn good behavior. Below are the cowboy rules of Roy Rogers, considered to be the King of Cowboys in Hollywood.

RIDER'S RULES BY ROY ROGERS

1. Be neat and clean.
2. Be courteous and polite.
3. Always obey your parents.
4. Protect the weak and help them.
5. Be brave but never take chances.
6. Study hard and learn all you can.
7. Be kind to animals and take care of them.
8. Eat all your food and never waste any.
9. Love God and go to Sunday school regularly.
10. Always respect our flag and our country.

COWBOY CLOTHES

"The Cow Boy" by J.C.H. Grabill, photographed at Sturgis, Dakota Territory, 1888

Everybody knows what a cowboy looks like. Tall 10-gallon hat on his head. Fancy shirt, leather chaps over his blue jeans, and of course, pointy-toed high-heeled cowboy boots. That's what all the cowboys wore, right?

Wrong.

That's the image of a movie or television cowboy. The real cowboys of the Old West never wore 10-gallon hats. That big hat would have stood out on the prairie like a bullseye on a target. Fancy shirts were only for rodeo shows, and blue jeans weren't invented until 1873.

So what did an 1860s-era cowboy look like? It depended on where he lived and what he could scrounge together. After the Civil War ended, times were hard and money was scarce. Cowboys wore what they had or what was cheap. Many of them had served in the military, so they wore the wool pants from their uniform and often the hat, shirt, and coat. As their uniforms wore out, they replaced them with whatever they could purchase at secondhand stores.

Chaps were leather leg coverings worn by the Spanish vaqueros. American cowboys started wearing chaps to protect their pants from being ripped by thorns and bushes. Torn and worn-out pants were a constant problem and the chuck wagon cook was often called upon to do the mending as well as the cooking.

The invention of thick denim pants held together by rivets was embraced by miners and cowboys across the West. When Levi Strauss introduced his new pants, they were an instant hit and quickly replaced the old wool pants. During the 1870s, economic times were better and cowboys could afford to replace their worn-out military uniforms with new mass-produced clothing.

Cowboys wore loose-fitting wool shirts. They needed long sleeves to protect their arms from scratches and sunburn. They often wore vests with pockets. It was pretty hard for cowboys to put their hands in their pants pockets when they were sitting on a horse. A vest made pockets accessible.

Hats were important to keep the sun and rain off the cowboy's head, but like the blue jean, the classic cowboy Stetson was not invented until 1865. Before that, the cowboys' favorite hat was a bowler or "derby." It had a narrow brim and low crown. It provided protection and stayed on the head when galloping on a horse.

The Stetson was introduced to the West in 1865. John B. Stetson had traveled west to improve his health. While he was in Colorado panning for gold, he made a hat for himself out of thick beaver felt. It had an extra wide brim to keep the sun out of his eyes and the rain off his face. The felt hat shed water much better than the bowler and could be molded into different shapes as needed. The hat had an extra tall crown to provide a pocket of air over the head for insulation from heat or cold.

It was an instant hit. Stetson's hats were not cheap, so a cowboy who could afford to buy a Stetson was showing the world that he was "doing well." By 1906, the Stetson Company was making nearly 2 million hats a year. The Stetson became known as the "Boss of the Plains."

Probably the most important piece of clothing that a cowboy owned was his boots. Real cowboys had their boots custom made. Any cowboy who didn't have custom-made boots was either not a real cowboy or was saving up to pay for his own custom boots.

The distinctive style of the boots had a purpose. The high heel kept the cowboy's foot from sliding forward in the stirrup and getting stuck. The pointed toe allowed the boot to slide easily in and out of the stirrup. Sometimes the sliding out was the most important part. If a cowboy was thrown from the horse, he wanted his foot to slide out of the stirrup so he would not be dragged behind the horse.

The tall shaft of the boot held the boot in place without laces. It also protected the calf and ankle from bushes, thorns, rocks, and snakebites. During wet weather or crossing streams, it kept water from flowing into the boot.

Many outfits worn by western reenactors are painstakingly researched, with these outfits ranging from 1865 to 1910

Most cowboy boots were dark leather and plain in style. The fancy colored and embroidered cowboy boots were an invention of Hollywood. Movie stars like Gene Autry and Roy Rogers were shown wearing brightly colored and elaborate cowboy boots. The cowboys of the 1800s would never have worn red or purple boots.

Bandannas were an essential part of the cowboy outfit. The square piece of cloth was typically folded into a triangle shape and tied around the neck. Extra bandannas were kept in a cowboy's vest pocket for emergency uses. Bandannas were used to mop sweat, to keep the sun or cold off the neck, and as dust masks. They were also used as bandages, tourniquets, and slings. They were an all-purpose tool.

LOYAL TO THE BRAND

"Branding calves on roundup" by John C. H. Grabill, 1888

When a cowboy talked about being loyal to the brand, he wasn't yakking about drinking Coke instead of Pepsi. He was talking about the brand on his cattle—the name of the ranch he worked for.

A branding iron was a solid metal rod with a symbol attached to the end. The symbol was heated in a fire until it was red hot. Then the branding iron was pressed into the hide of the cow. The symbol or brand identified whose cow was whose.

In the American West in the 1800s, cattle ranged free without fences. The only way to tell your cattle from your neighbors was by the brand on their hips. Each ranch designed its own distinctive brand and cowboys were loyal to their brand and ranch.

Branding was not invented by the American cowboy. Hieroglyphics on Egyptian tombs show that oxen were branded as early as 2700 B.C. European countries that raised large herds of cattle, like Spain, also practiced branding. The Spanish brought the tradition with them when they settled in the Americas.

Branding helped protect the herd from cattle rustlers. Rancher knew their neighbors' brands and they honored those brands. It was against their code to try to take another person's cattle and claim it or sell it. If a cattle rustler was caught trying to sell another rancher's cattle, he would certainly go to jail and might be strung up on a rope necktie.

Some crafty rustlers tried to alter the brands on the cattle. They would "rebrand" the cows—adding a line, bar, or circle to make the brand look like a different ranch's mark. Sometimes this worked, and other times they got caught. But it was risky. Branding took time and the longer the rustler kept the cattle without selling them, the more likely he was to be caught.

Ranchers and cowboys all knew how to read the brands on cattle.

Ƨ	A letter that was upside down was a "crazy" letter. For example an upside down S would be "crazy S."
∽	A letter turned sideways was called lazy. An S on its side was "lazy S."
S̄	A line over the top of a letter was read as a "bar." Two lines above an S would be read as "2 bar S."

HERE ARE SOME RANCHES AND THEIR BRANDS

Flying P	
Flying O	
N Bar N	
Circle L Bar	
Bar Y Bar	
Lazy E	
Lazy BW	
Four Sixes	
M Six	

Swinging R	℞
Rocking H	Ⱨ
Chain C	Ꝑ
Double H	HH
Four E	4E
Y Cross	Ұ
R Arrow	R→

Sometimes cowboys made jokes with brand symbols. What does this brand say?

Answer: Too lazy to pee.

COWPOKE PRACTICE
Brand It

You can create your own brand and keep rustlers out of your room. Just take a look at the branding alphabet at http://www.tscrabrands.com/design-brand.html for inspiration. Then design a brand with your name, your initials, or your own unique symbols.

Materials

- ❑ Scissors
- ❑ Pencil
- ❑ Paper
- ❑ Craft foam
- ❑ Washable paint
- ❑ Paper plate
- ❑ Craft stick

First, decide how you want your brand to look. Draw it in the area provided on the next page.

Lay the paper backward on the craft foam and trace your brand on to the foam with your pencil. Then cut out the brand.

Next place some washable paint on the paper plate. Spread it around with the craft stick so it is even. Then dip your brand into the paint. You will use it as a stamp on paper or cloth. Make sure you have your family's permission before you do any branding!

This can get a little messy, so you may want to have some wet paper towels on hand for clean up. Have fun branding your ranch!

YOUR BRAND DESIGN

COWPOKE PRACTICE
Chuck Wagon Recipes

Hey pardner! Round up an adult family member to help you make some bang-up recipes that are sure to make your belly happy.

COWBOY FRY BREAD

Ingredients

- ❏ 1 cup milk
- ❏ 1 package active dry yeast
- ❏ 2 tablespoons sugar
- ❏ 2 cackleberries (eggs) beaten
- ❏ 1 teaspoon salt
- ❏ 3 1/2 cups flour, sifted
- ❏ Vegetable oil

Heat the milk until warm but not hot. Pour it into a large bowl and add the yeast and sugar. Stir in those cackleberries and salt. Then slowly mix the flour in. Don't go too fast, buckaroo, or you'll make a heck of a mess.

When it is well-mixed and the dough is stretchy, cover it with a towel and set it aside for 30 minutes to an hour. When the dough has risen to twice its size, it's ready for workin'.

Lightly flour your work surface and divide the dough into 12 pieces the size of tennis balls. Flatten them out and let 'em rise again. This should only take about 10 minutes.

Have that adult buckaroo heat up the vegetable oil to 350 degrees in a large pot or skillet. Fry the dough pieces one or two at a time for 3–5 minutes. Then enjoy some tasty chow.

Chuck wagon on a Texas roundup, 1900

VINEGAR PIE

When the cowboys got a hankerin' for somethin' sweet, cook would make this recipe.

Ingredients

❑ 1 cup sugar

❑ 2 tablespoons flour

❑ 1 cup cold water

❑ 4 cackleberries (eggs, remember!) beaten

❑ Uncooked store-bought piecrust (we're cheatin' here!)

❑ 5 tablespoons vinegar (vinegar was used in the West to give the cowboys some vitamin C)

❑ 2 1/2 tablespoons butter

Mix up the sugar and flour in a saucepan. Then add the rest of the ingredients. Cook on medium heat until thick. Then pour into the waiting piecrust. Bake in the oven at 375 degrees until the crust is golden brown. Then dig in!

LEGENDS AND LORE

The Overland Pony Express illustrated in *Harper's Weekly*, 1867

This is the advertisement that everybody associates with the Pony Express. Legend has it that the Pony Express preferred orphans because its organizers couldn't be sure if the riders would survive the trip. But truth is, there is no evidence that this advertisement ever existed and fortunately almost all of the riders survived their adventure.

Stories of the Pony Express and wild rides across the West are plentiful. The problem is figuring out which ones are true. Buffalo Bill's traveling show featured riders from the Pony Express who told tales of terror from their days on the trail—those are the stories that people have told and retold. But Buffalo Bill's show was *entertainment* and some of the stories were just tall tales. As one old saying puts it, "Out West we don't lie . . . we just remember big."

Historians have done their best to research and find out the real facts about the Pony Express. Some of those stories are just as frightening as the myths. Here's the real scoop on the legendary Pony Express.

The Pony Express began April 3, 1860, and only operated for 19 months. The goal of the business was to get mail from the eastern United States to California as fast as possible. In 1860, the rail and telegraph lines didn't reach all the way to the West Coast. Mail was often transported by train as far as St. Joseph, MO. From there, letters and newspapers traveled by stagecoach to California. It could take months for people to receive news, letters, or business contracts from the East Coast, if they received them at all. With stagecoach robberies and mishaps, sometimes the mail never reached its destination.

The founders of the Pony Express knew they could improve on the current system. They decided to develop a mail relay where a rider would gallop at full speed for 10 to 12 miles from one station to the next. That was as long as a horse could last at full speed. At each station, there was a fresh horse

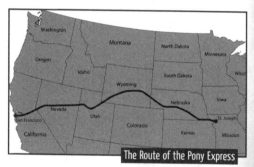

The Route of the Pony Express

waiting. The rider would take the mail pouch, transfer to the fresh horse, and ride off again. Each rider covered between 75 and 100 miles in a day. It took a mere 10 days to get the mail from St. Joseph, MO, to Sacramento, CA. It was considered an amazing feat in 1860.

Sending a letter with the Pony Express was not cheap. When the Express started, the cost was $5 for a 1/2 ounce letter. That would be equal $130 in today's money. It would have to be a very important letter to Grandma for that much money! By the end of the Pony Express, the cost was a bargain at only $1 per 1/2 ounce (only $26 in today's money).

Legend has it that riders were all in their teens, but that's not true either. There was one 11-year-old who rode at least one leg of the journey and one man who was in his forties. Age was not as important as how well the riders knew the trail and how much he weighed. No rider could be heavier than 120 pounds. Galloping horses needed to have a little weight as possible on their back. Saddles were made lighter and the mailbag could only contain 20 pounds of mail. The only thing the rider carried besides the mail was water and a revolver.

One of the most terrifying rides was completed by Robert Haslam. The 20-year-old Haslam left on May 10, 1860, from San Francisco and headed east with the mail packet. But when he arrived at Buckland Station, he found the relief rider there was so scared of the Paiute Indian War that he refused to ride. Haslam felt it was his duty to continue on with the mail. He

Buffalo Bill and the Pony Express

One of the youngest riders on the Pony Express was William Cody. At 14, he was recruited to ride for the mail delivery system. He was young, thin, and an experienced horseman. Later Bill Cody organized a Wild West Show that traveled around the world telling about the adventures of cowboys and the Pony Express. Buffalo Bill's Wild West Show was more like a circus than a stage show and included a parade on horseback, cowboys and American Indian performers, and shooting demonstrations. It was a long way from his days of galloping on the trail with a pouch of mail.

rode 190 miles at a full gallop with no rest. Finally he reached Smith's Creek and slept for 9 hours.

But his ride wasn't over. Haslam was given the westbound mail at Smith's Creek and had to turn around and ride back the way he came—right through the Paiute Indian War. Haslam mounted his pony and took off. He made it to Cold Springs, but found the stationmaster dead and all of the stock captured by the Paiutes.

Haslam kept riding. He was ambushed by the Paiute and shot in the jaw with an arrow. He still kept riding. Bleeding and exhausted, he finally made it back to Buckland's Station— where he delivered a copy of President Lincoln's Inaugural Address. A doctor patched him up, but he lost three teeth from the arrow wound. His ride had been 380 miles and was the longest ride of anyone in the Pony Express.

On October 24, 1961, the transcontinental telegraph reached Salt Lake City, UT, and completed the connection of the East Coast with California. Now telegrams could be sent from New York to Sacramento. The Pony Express was no longer needed, and it closed 2 days later. The Pony Express was only in business for 19 months, but its riders delivered 35,000 letters between Missouri and California.

Assortment of postmarks used on Pony Express mail, 1860

THE LOST DUTCHMAN'S GOLD MINE

Jacob Waltz lay dying. His breathing was shallow and the words he mumbled were hard to understand. He kept muttering about the mine, the gold, and the mountains. Julia Thomas wiped the old man's face and tried to keep him comfortable. There wasn't much else she could do to help but listen to his ramblings and wonder if any of the stories were true.

Waltz was known as a reclusive old miner. He emigrated from Germany to Arizona in the 1870s and went to work at the Vulture gold mine. There he met another miner named Jacob Weiser. The two became friends and eventually they decided they would try making their own fortune by looking for gold in the Superstition Mountains.

For centuries, stories had been told about an incredibly rich gold mine hidden in the deep crevices of the rugged peaks. The Native Americans considered the mountains to be sacred ground and believed that the thunder god would take revenge on anyone who defiled the land.

When Spanish conquistadors arrive in 1540, they didn't care about the warnings from the Apache leaders. They began searching the mountains for gold, silver, and other minerals. But strange things began to happen. Soldiers began to disappear. Soon so many soldiers were lost that the men were warned to never stray more than a few feet from the group.

Later they began finding the lost men. They were dead and their heads had been cut off. The conquistadors refused to stay on the mountains and gave the range the name Monte Superstition.

Nearly 200 years later, Don Miguel Peralta, a Mexican cattle baron, began ranching in the area. His family explored the area extensively and found rich deposits of both gold and silver. This was the first historical recording of the gold mine. His family understood how much the Apache Nation disliked having the mountain disturbed so they made infrequent trips to the mine, bringing out as much ore as they could carry.

This method worked for the Peralta family for nearly 100 years. But in 1846, four of the Peralta descendants got greedy. They mined as much as they could and hauled it out. They took a herd of mules and wagons to the mine and loaded up bags of gold. Worried that somebody might stumble upon their mine while they were gone, they concealed the entrance so it could not be easily identified. Then they set out for Mexico.

They never made it home.

The Apache leaders were angry because their sacred ground had been violated. The Peralta men and the miners were killed. The donkeys and mules ran from the scene, spilling gold across the desert ground.

It was 30 years later that Jacob Waltz and his friend Jacob Weiser somehow met one of the Peralta heirs. Some stories say that they saved Peralta from a knife fight and in gratitude he gave them a map to the mine. Other stories say they stole the map and others say they just got lucky and stumbled upon the mine. No one knows for sure, but somehow the two Jacobs found a huge amount of gold.

In 1877, the two men showed up in Phoenix and bought supplies with very high-grade gold ore. They never told anyone where they found it, and they never filed a claim. For several years, the two men would disappear for months at a time only to show up with bags full of rich ore.

Eventually Jacob Weiser stopped showing up in town. Nobody knew for sure what happened to him and Jacob Waltz never explained. People suspected Waltz may have killed him, but there was nobody to prove he was actually dead.

Waltz kept disappearing and returning with gold. People tried to follow him, but he was always able to lose them in the mountain trails. Then in 1891, Waltz became ill. He was an elderly man in his eighties. Julia Thomas was called in to nurse him.

Julia was aware of the stories about Waltz, and she tried to listen to the old man's rambling words. She had help in listening from Herman and Reinhardt Petrasch, neighbors of Waltz's. They took notes and tried to make sense of his directions.

After Waltz died, the three set out to find the mine. They

searched for 5 weeks, but never found anything. From that point on, the gold mine was referred to as the Lost Dutchman's Mine, even though Waltz was of German and not Dutch descent. Hundreds of people have wandered through the Superstition Mountains looking for the lost treasure, but none have found it yet. Some people think the real question is whether there ever actually was a treasure to begin with or if it is all just legend and rumor.

Can You Solve the Mystery?

Legend has it that the Peralta family left a clue to the location of the mine carved into some red sandstone tablets. For years, treasure hunters have tried to decipher the stones and find the treasure. Take a look at the stones and see if you can figure out if they are clues to treasure or an elaborate hoax.

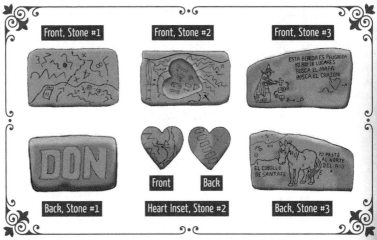

Front, Stone #1

Front, Stone #2

Front, Stone #3

Back, Stone #1

Heart Inset, Stone #2

Back, Stone #3

RATTLESNAKE DICK'S LOOT

Rattlesnake Dick was a man with a plan. A really bad plan.

Rattlesnake Dick (a.k.a. Richard Barter) started out as a California gold miner, but he wasn't very good at it. He thought maybe he'd be better at stealing horses, but he got caught and sent to jail for 2 years.

When he got out of jail, he decided he would form a gang of outlaws and they could make their fortune robbing gold shipments. His plan was to steal the gold off the pack mules as they came down Trinity Mountain from the gold mines. But Rattlesnake Dick just wasn't very good at planning.

He thought it would be good idea to get some extra mules to help them carry their stolen gold. He set off with Cy Skinner and the two of them went to steal some mules while the rest of the gang robbed the gold shipment.

Rattlesnake Dick got caught, again. He was sitting in jail for trying to steal mules when his friends successfully robbed the gold shipment. They made off with $80,000 worth of gold (that would be more than $1.5 million dollars in today's money), but because Rattlesnake had never shown up with the extra mules, the gang had a hard time carrying all that heavy gold.

They decided to bury half of the gold and made their way down the mountain with the other half. Before they had a chance to spend a dime, they were caught by a Wells Fargo posse. A gunfight ensued, one that didn't end well for the robbers. In no time at all, half the gold was sent right back to its rightful owners. The other half was still hidden in the mountains. None of the Wells Fargo lawmen could find the missing gold.

When Rattlesnake Dick was released from jail for trying to steal the mules, he headed straight up the mountain to look for that missing gold. He searched for weeks, but couldn't find it. He gave up and decided he'd try a new venture—stagecoach hold-ups. He was just as successful with that as he was with everything else: He was shot and killed by Sheriff J. Boggs.

Rattlesnake Dick's gold loot has never been found. Legend says that it is still on Trinity Mountain buried about 12 miles from the point of the robbery. But so far, none of the treasure hunters have had better luck than Rattlesnake Dick.

U.S. CAMEL CORPS

Members of the US Camel Corps in the southwestern desert, 1857

It seemed like a good idea at the time. It was hot and dry in the Southwest. Horses need water, but camels—well, they are used to deserts. Why not just buy a few camels and let the soldiers use them instead of horses? It worked in Egypt, didn't it?

In 1855, the Southwestern part of America was difficult to reach. Trains didn't go that far west and automobiles hadn't been invented. Horses and mules were used to pull wagons and coaches, but they needed a constant supply of water. And water was hard to come by. Hauling enough water for the troops and their horses made for very heavy loads. It was especially a problem for the Army.

Jefferson Davis, the newly appointed Secretary of State, was sure that camels were the solution. They worked in the Sahara Desert, where there was even less water than the American Southwest. Davis proposed to Congress that it should at least experiment with camels. He argued the facts, comparing camels to horses: Camels could carry 700–900 pounds of supplies and can travel 30–40 miles a day. Camels are able to survive without water and food for 8 days, and their feet are adapted to rough rocky terrain. They do not need to be shoed like a horse.

Alternatively, horses must be shoed in order to keep their hooves from splitting on the hard rocks. They can only carry 250–300 pounds and they need to be watered two to three times a day. A horse will die from dehydration in 3 days.

Davis's arguments were convincing. Congress set aside $30,000 to purchase camels for the Army. The great camel experiment had begun.

Davis appointed Major Henry C. Wayne, another camel enthusiast, to purchase the camels. The camel-buying team took a ship and headed for North Africa. They ran into numerous problems while trying to purchase the camels. They were often offered sick or diseased animals. They had to search to find honest camel sellers and good stock. Then they had to get export permits. It took 5 months to purchase 33 camels at the cost of $250 per animal. A horse could be purchased for $50.

When Major Wayne arrived at Camp Verde in Texas with his herd of camels, the soldiers were not impressed. The camels smelled strange and scared the soldiers' horses. Camels, like cows, regurgitate their food and chew it over and over again—called chewing their cud. But when the camels got mad, they would spit the cud at the soldiers. The soliders hated being covered in green camel slobber.

It wasn't until the soldiers tested the camels out in the field that they appreciated the camel's unique talents. The soldiers and camels were sent on a surveying expedition. At first, the soldiers complained about the camels, their smell, and their strange way of walking. They were so different from the horses.

But after a few weeks, the soldiers changed their minds. The camels could carry far more weight than either horses or mules and moved at a faster pace. The camels ate the prickly bushes that the horses and mules wouldn't touch. They didn't need water and could easily travel 40 miles a day.

Once, a survey party got lost in an impassable canyon. They wandered for 36 hours without food or water. The horses and mules were frantic, but the camels were calm. Some of the soldiers decided to take a small group of the camels on a scouting party to see if they could find water. The camels located a river 20 miles from the canyon and led the rest of the troops to it. The camels saved the lives of the soldiers and the other animals.

For the next several years, the camels were used for survey expeditions, but even though they were proven to be successful, many soldiers still rebelled at the thought of riding a camel off to war. It just didn't seem dignified. So the camels were just used for special tasks.

In 1861, the Civil War started and Camp Verde was taken over by Confederate troops. The Confederate soldiers had no idea how useful the camels were. They were scared of the large animals and didn't know how to handle them. This, of course, made the camels angry. The camels kicked and spit at the Confederate soldiers. The soldiers abused the camels and even killed some of them. Eventually the camels were either sold or let loose into the desert to fend for themselves.

The camels did well in the desert and actually multiplied. For several decades, people reported seeing camels wandering the Mojave Desert. The last reported sighting was in the middle of the 20th century—nearly 100 years after the camels were first brought to America.

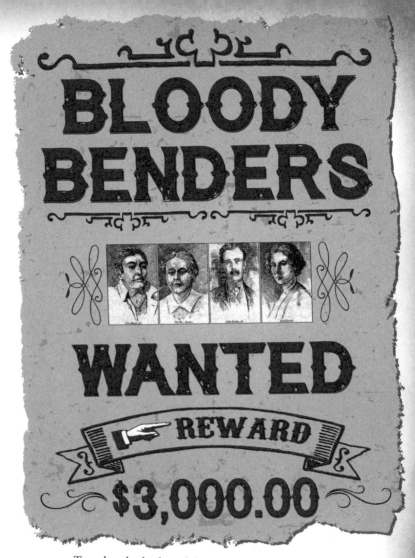

BLOODY BENDERS

WANTED

REWARD

$3,000.00

Travelers had a lot of things to worry about in the wilds of the West. They could be attacked by robbers, mauled by wild animals, or die from heat stroke and lack of water. That's why guesthouses were so popular. Ranchers and farmers who opened up their homes to weary travelers were deeply appreciated and were paid for their safe beds and warm food. But a stay at the Benders' guesthouse was more dangerous than supper with a grizzly bear.

The Bender family moved to Kansas in 1870 and settled near the Osage Trail. They built a home that had a small store in the front. They also offered lodgings to people traveling the trail. Ma and Pa Bender spoke mostly German, but their two adult children spoke fluent English.

Kate Bender lived with her parents on their homestead and her brother, John, claimed the homestead next to his parents. Kate was said to be pretty, charming, and a spiritualist who could tell fortunes, see into the future, and heal sickness.

Kate used her supernatural skills to bring business to her family. She had flyers printed up and distributed advertising herself as Professor Bender. She advertised that she could "Cure all sorts of diseases; can cure blindness, fits, deafness and all such disease, also deaf and dumbness."

As Professor Miss Kate Bender she traveled to towns in Kansas and performed séances. People were impressed at how should could summon up ghosts and speak to them. Because she was pretty she had many male admirers, and these men would stop by the Bender place for supper and a private séance show.

If the visitor was wealthy, Kate would sit him in a place of honor at the head of the table. The dining room was divided from the rest of the house by thick cloth canvas. The visitor would sit with his back to the canvas.

With the visitor seated in that perfect spot, Miss Kate was able to make all sorts of spirits speak and ghostly apparitions show themselves. Of course, behind the canvas her family was hard at work supplying sounds and ghostly movements.

Kate made money from her séances, her family made money from the travelers staying with them, and for a while, people just thought they were a strange family but not a real problem. Most of the neighbors just left them alone.

But in the winter of 1872, a man named George Newton Longcor and his infant daughter were traveling the Osage Trail to resettle in Iowa, but they never reached their destination.

Longcor's neighbor, Dr. William York, decided to investigate what had happened to his friend and small daughter. He set out to trace their path on the Osage Trail. Along the way, he questioned people and tried to stay where his friend might have stayed. Dr. York wrote to his brother Colonel Ed York about his travels. But when the letters stopped and Dr. York never came home, his brother became quite suspicious.

The colonel mounted up a party of 50 men and they began a search along the trail asking everybody if they had seen the doctor. When the colonel's men arrived at the Bender home, the family talked to the colonel and suggested that maybe the doctor had simply been delayed in his travels. Kate offered to hold a séance to see if the spirits could help them find the missing doctor.

A few days later, Colonel York heard about a woman who claimed to have been threated by Ma Bender with a knife. The woman said she had been terrified that they were going to kill her.

When Ma Bender was asked about it, she said that the woman was a witch who had cursed her coffee. Now the colonel was getting really suspicious and he obtained a search warrant to look into every homestead in the area.

But by the time the warrant was issued and Colonel York and his men returned, the Benders were gone. The house was empty. There were no clothes, food, or any personal possessions left. The only thing left was a very terrible odor.

The smell was traced to a trap door underneath a bed. When the colonel's men opened up the trap door, they found nothing but a stone slab that seemed to be covered in dried blood. The men dug up the whole area around the slab, but did not find any bodies.

The evidence of the blood made every one believe they would find the body of Dr. York and quite possibly Mr. Longcor and his baby girl. They lifted up the entire cabin and dug under it, but didn't find anything. Then, they started hunting through the vegetable garden. There they found Dr. York's body. Soon they uncovered the body of Mr. Longcor, his baby girl buried underneath him. As the men kept digging, they found another body and then another. By the time they were finished, they found 10 bodies buried in the Bender yard.

The settlers were horrified. How could their neighbors have done something so terrible and why? None of the travelers was carrying large amounts of money. The Benders were certainly not getting rich from their killings. Newspapers across the country carried stories about the grisly murders. A reward of $3,000 was offered for the capture of the Benders. No one ever collected the reward. Law officials believe that the Benders escaped simply by purchasing train tickets.

The story of the Bloody Benders became Wild West legend. This was one of the first times a serial murder had been committed in the American West, and it was a crime that would go unsolved.

GUNFIGHT AT THE O.K. CORRAL

The newspapers told the story with graphic pictures. Three dead men, their corpses propped up for the photographer, made the front page of newspapers across America. It was the gunfight at the O.K. Corral and it became the stuff of Wild West legend. But how much of the story is true? And what was the fight really about?

Most people think of the shootout at the O.K. Corral happening in a dusty ghost town, but in 1861, Tombstone, AZ, was a bustling town full of modern conveniences and luxuries. It was a silver mining town that brought up $37 million worth of silver ore. In today's money, that would equal $8.2 billion.

The miners worked day and night and stores, banks, and restaurants were open 24 hours a day to service them. The business owners were making vast amounts of money and they could buy everything from the finest silk for dresses to fresh seafood caught in California and shipped by wagon every day. The townspeople had a theatre hall with opera performances. There was a bowling alley, a luxury hotel, and the town even boasted some of the newfangled telephones.

The business people aspired for Tombstone to be a reputable town, so one of the rules they wanted enforced was that no guns be allowed in the city limits. That's another thing that surprises people. We think that cowboys rode through town shooting in the air and getting into gunfights. In truth, that was the last thing the people of Tombstone wanted. To keep the peace, they hired the Earp brothers to act as the town's lawmen. One of the Earps' toughest jobs was to make sure cowboys who came into town did not bring their guns with them.

Virgil Earp was the town marshal and he had his brother, Morgan, working for him as the assistant town marshal. Wyatt Earp was a deputy marshal. They had several disagreements with cowboys before the gunfight at the O.K. Corral occurred. Wyatt Earp had actually identified and arrested some of the cowboys for robbing stagecoaches. Of course, the cowboys then said that it was really Wyatt who had done the robbing. There was no love lost between the cowboy gang and the Earp brothers.

On the night of October 25, 1881, the cowboy leader, Ike Clanton, got into a fight with the Earps' friend Doc Holliday. The next day, Clanton roamed up and down the street where Doc lived and threatened to kill him.

Virgil Earp heard about the commotion and was informed that a group of cowboys was armed and waiting for Doc Holliday outside his house. Virgil knew he had to disarm the cowboys before something happened. He gathered his brothers and deputized Doc and headed out to see what was happening.

By the time they reached the O.K. Corral, the cowboys had walked on over to a vacant lot. Virgil's intent was still to simply take the guns away and hopefully avoid any more problems. But when Virgil announced that he was there to take away the cowboys' guns, two of the cowboys fired.

As soon as they heard gunshots, the Earp brothers and Doc Holliday returned fire. Thirty seconds later, three of the cowboy gang were dead. Virgil, Morgan, and Doc Holliday had also been shot.

Movies show the Earp brothers being celebrated as heroes that saved the town, but the truth is that the Earp brothers and Doc were arrested and charged with murder. A month later, they were all found not guilty. The ruling was that they were "fully justified" in their actions.

The Earp brothers continued their work as lawmen and both Virgil and Morgan were killed in the line of duty. Doc Holliday died of tuberculosis. Only Wyatt lived to old age and died in California at the age of 80.

The First Telephones

The telephone was invented in 1876 and a telephone was installed in the White House in 1879. Deadwood, SD, had a telephone exchange installed in its town in 1878. Phone calls to the neighboring town of Lead cost 50 cents. That was 25 cents cheaper than a stagecoach ride and a whole lot less bumpy and dusty.

An actor portraying Alexander Graham Bell speaking into an early model telephone

COWPOKE PRACTICE
Lost Treasure Map

The Wild West is full of legends about lost and buried treasure. Sometimes robbers hid their treasures and others were lost mines of gold or silver. If only someone had created a map!

If you had to bury a treasure and didn't want anybody to figure out your secret, how could you make a map? If you put directions on it or wrote our words like "go south 25 yards from the big tree," anyone could figure out your map and steal your treasure. That is why some mapmakers used hieroglyphics—pictures that tell a story. Ancient people used hieroglyphics to tell stories and give directions. Many of these were discovered by explorers in Western America.

You can use your own set of hieroglyphics to make a treasure map. Think about a great hiding place. Maybe it is somewhere in your home or neighborhood. Then make a map to remind you where you have hidden your treasure.

Materials

☐ paper ☐ pencil

Think about using symbols instead of words. You can draw stairs instead of writing the word. How could you show crossing a stream or walking outside? Draw landmarks like tall trees, a fence, or a hole in the ground. Make sure your landmarks are something that will stay in the same place for a long period of time. Your dad might move his car or your mom might rearrange the furniture.

Once you have figured out your symbols, make your map. Then keep the map in a safe place. If you are worried that you might forget what your symbols mean, make a key for your map, but don't store the key and the map in the same place. Keep them separate. It will make it harder for someone to steal your treasure.

COWPOKE PRACTICE
Hangman Game

Sometimes games have some strange origins. Most people have played the word game Hangman but they may not have thought about where it came from. The history of the game dates back to Victorian times and was once called "Gallows."

In the 1800s, people were punished for murder by public hangings, or hanging from the gallows. Crowds of people actually watched when Wild West outlaws were hung. The gallows was such a common sight that it was turned into a child's spelling game.

Today teachers and parents think the game is too scary for kids to play, so they often change the gallows to apples on a tree. But it would have been common for children in the West to play the game Hangman.

If you want to, you can try the Hangman spelling game, but check with your family to see that it's okay with them.

Materials

- ❏ pencil
- ❏ paper
- ❏ at least one friend

Draw a gallows like the one below or use the one on the following page, then select one person to be the executioner. That person will think of a secret word or phrase and write out blanks for the letters in each word. Separate each word with a slash or a wide gap so the players will know how many letters are in each word.

The other players will take turns guessing letters of the alphabet. If the letter is in the word, then it gets written in the correct space. If the letter is not in the answer, then a body part gets added to the gallows (for example, the head, body, left arm, right arm, etc.) If the player guesses the word or phrase before the whole body is drawn on the gallows, the player wins. If not, the body is hung and the executioner wins.

GUESSES: A B E I D L

Draw the word or phrase blanks here:

C O W B O Y

Example of the Hangman game

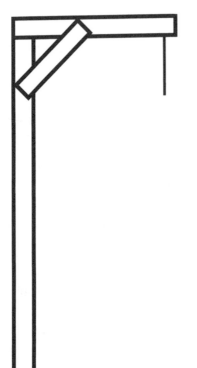

GUESSES: _____

_____

Draw the word or phrase blanks here:

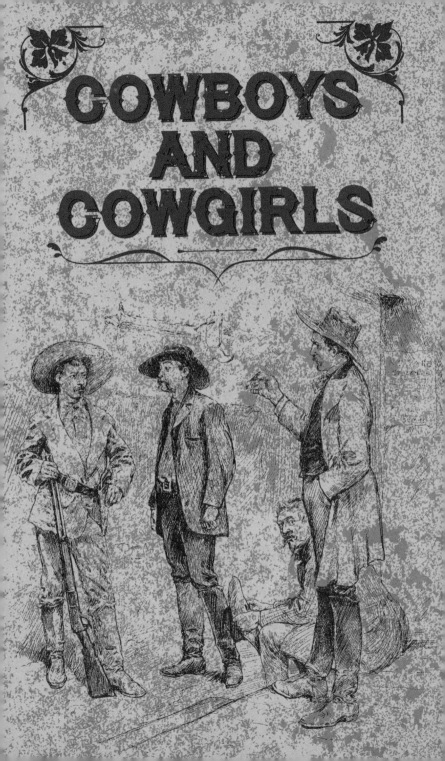

DEADWOOD DICK

Nat Love stood calmly in front of the trail boss and asked for a job. The boss stared at the skinny 16-year-old. What was this kid thinking? Did he have any idea how hard life was on the cattle trail? Did he know anything about horses at all? The trail boss shook his head. What the heck, he'd give the kid a chance. The boss pointed to a horse in the corral and said, "If you can break that horse, you've got a job." Nat grinned. Horse breaking was his specialty. He jumped into the corral and went to work.

It was a rough ride with the horse bucking and twisting to throw Nat off its back, but Nat held on like he had done many times before on the plantation where he grew up. Born a slave in 1854, Nat was raised around horses and had a special knack for knowing how to tame the wild ones. After Abraham Lincoln signed the Emancipation Proclamation, freeing the slaves, Nat and his family worked on a rented farm. He learned about farming and raising farm animals, but his real joy was horses. And at 16, he headed west to Dodge City to see if he could become a cowboy.

When the trail boss saw that Nat had tamed the wild horse, Nat had a job. He was signed on as a ranch hand at the Duval Ranch and was paid $30 a month. Nat felt like he was in heaven. He quickly learned the cowboy skills of roping, tying, and shooting. He was good at all of them, but he was especially good at shooting. He practiced shooting a .45 revolver at targets and competing against the other cowboys. Pretty soon, Nat could outshoot them all.

In the spring of 1876, Nat's crew was sent to Deadwood, SD, to deliver a herd of 3,000 cattle. When the cowboys arrived, the town was getting ready for its Fourth of July celebration. The young cowboys were happy to join in the competition. There were roping contests, and tying, bridle, and riding competitions, as well as shooting contests. By the end of the day, Nat Love had won every single event. The townspeople adored Nat and happily awarded him the $200 prize. They also gave him the nickname he would carry for the rest of his life, Deadwood Dick.

The Life and Adventures of Nat Love

You can read Nat's autobiography at http://docsouth.unc.edu/neh/natlove/menu.html

A year later, Love was captured by a band of Pima Indians. Love eventually stole a pony and managed to escape. He felt the only reason they did not kill him was because they admired his fighting skills.

Nat spent another 15 years working as a cowboy. He traveled frequently to Mexico and became fluent in Spanish. He used his skills as a marksman to fight off rustlers and protect his cattle from predators. In 1889, he decided it was time to settle down. He married and took a job working on the railroad. Even though he had been born a slave, Nat's father had made sure Nat could read and write. After his retirement from ranch life he wrote his autobiography, titled *The Life and Adventures of Nat Love, Better Known in the Cattle Country as Deadwood Dick*. It was an instant hit, and people all over the United States were fascinated with Nat Love, the cowboy. Nat died in 1927 at the age of 67, but his story lives on in history.

BUFFALO BILL

ADVENTURES OF
BUFFALO BILL

HIS INDIAN BATTLES, LAST HUNTING
TRIP WITH THE PRINCE OF MONACO,
OWNER OF MONTE CARLO, AND INCIDENTS
OF HIS HOME LIFE.

Essanay

It was dry and dusty on the trail as Billy prodded his pony with his heels to make him trot. The pony wanted to walk like all of the other horses in the wagon train, but Billy had to keep his pony moving so he could deliver the message from the trail boss to the workers at the rear of the convoy.

It was Billy's first job, and he was proud to be able to earn money to help his family. When is father died in 1857, Billy was just 11 years old. As the oldest son, Billy knew it was his responsibility to go to work to earn money for his family, and he signed on with a freight carrier as a "boy extra."

He began traveling with the freight company from his home in Ft. Leavenworth, KS, across the plains of Nebraska into Colorado and Wyoming. He was gone from his mother and family for months at a time. Along the way, he learned how to handle a team of horses and how to drive oxen. He saw Native Americans hunting on the prairies and watched buffalo grazing in the grasslands.

When Billy wasn't working on the freight train, he earned money by trapping animals for fur and recovering stray or stolen horses for the Army at Ft. Leavenworth. In between, he attended school, although that wasn't his favorite occupation. He tried the patience of the teacher, who wore out several switches trying to keep Billy's attention focused on his books.

By the time he was 14, Billy was an experienced horseman, trapper, and frontiersman. He was earning $40 per month and having his paychecks sent home. It was enough money to take care of his mother and sisters. Billy was successful.

Then he saw an advertisement that offered to pay $100 a month to ride a horse. Billy knew he was right for the job and signed on to ride for the Pony Express. Riding hard and fast, Billy raced with mailbags through freezing blizzards and sweltering heat. He became tougher and stronger, but his mother grew sicker and weaker. Billy left the Pony Express when he got word that his mother was dying. She passed away in 1863. Billy grieved. And then he went back to work.

This time he enlisted in the Union Army. He became Private Bill Cody and served in the Seventh Kansas Volunteer Cavalry. The cavalry suited Bill. He served until the end of the war and then worked off and on for the cavalry as a scout for the next 9 years.

It was during this time that Bill earned his famous nickname. Bill had a contract to provide meat for the Kansas railroad workers, and in 18 months' time, he claimed he killed 4,280 head of buffalo. That was a lot of meat for a lot of hungry men. The Kansas Pacific Railroad workers were so impressed with his hunting abilities that they made up a song.

> Buffalo Bill, Buffalo Bill
> He never missed and he never will
> Always aims and shoots to kill
> And the company pays his buffalo bill.

The stories of Buffalo Bill and his adventures caught the attention of a writer named E. Z. C. Judson. His stories about Buffalo Bill were featured in the *New York Weekly*. The people back east wanted to learn more about the hunting, riding, and fighting adventures of Buffalo Bill. Judson obliged them by writing a play titled "Scouts of the Prairie." Judson invited Buffalo Bill to star as himself in the play. The critics hated it, but the people loved it. The play was a success, and it gave Buffalo Bill an idea.

People loved hearing the stories about Native Americans. They wanted to learn about cattle ranching and the lives of cowboys and cowgirls. Buffalo Bill decided to start his own show. He called on his old friends, Wild Bill Hickok and Texas Jack Omohundro to join him in telling stories of the Wild West. Buffalo Bill and his friends performed on stage during the winter season and then returned to their hunting and scouting in good weather. He toured on stage for 11 seasons.

But Buffalo Bill had ideas for a Wild West show that was bigger than any stage could contain. He wanted to have cowboys riding real horses and roping real cows. He wanted to show the skills of hunters with real sharpshooters and real bullets. On July 4, 1883, Buffalo Bill staged the "Wild West, Rocky Mountain, and Prairie Exhibition" extravaganza in North Platte, NE. It was an instant success.

Audiences loved watching cowboys demonstrate rope tricks and cheered at live demonstrations of the Pony Express relay. They peeked between their fingers to see if Annie Oakley could really shoot the cigar out of a man's mouth and sighed with relief when she was successful. For the next 4 years, Buffalo Bill and his Wild West show toured America. Then he took the show to Europe.

Queen Victoria attended two command performances. Heads of state, presidents, and movie stars all went to see Buffalo Bill's show. It was so popular that Buffalo Bill and his show toured the world for 30 years. The last performance was in 1913. But even then, Buffalo Bill didn't stop. He continued to tell his stories on stage until 2 months before he died in 1917.

His funeral was as popular as one of his shows. There were 18,000 people who paid tribute to the man who had popularized the West. Years later, historians would argue that Buffalo Bill presented a romanticized version of the West. Many of his stage stories were not factual or were heavily embellished to make the show more interesting. But Buffalo Bill was successful in helping people learn about Western culture and without his shows, many of the stories might have been lost to history.

Sharpshooter Annie Oakley

Watch the Wild West Show

You can watch real videos of Buffalo Bill and his Wild West show filmed by Thomas Edison. Take a look at https://www.youtube.com/watch?v=3w__1GyfQPQ

CHARLEY PARKHURST

Indians attacking a stagecoach in the Far West

He was known as one of the best "whips," or stagecoach drivers, in the country. Wiry and strong, Charley Parkhurst knew how to manage a team of six racing horses, fight off robbers, and make the customers happy. He was a gun-carrying, cigar-smoking cowboy who knew how to repair just about every part on a stagecoach.

For 30 years, Charley drove stagecoaches in California. He became known as one of Wells Fargo's fastest and safest drivers, delivering passengers from Stockton to Mariposa and

OVERLAND MAIL ROUTE
TO CALIFORNIA.
Through in Six Days to Sacramento!

CONNECTING WITH THE DAILY STAGES
To all the Interior Mining Towns in Northern California and Southern Oregon.
Ticketed through from Portland, by the

OREGON LINE OF STAGE COACHES!
And the Rail Road from Oroville to Sacramento,

Passing through Oregon City, Salem, Albany, Corvallis, Eugene City, Oakland,
Winchester, Roseburg, Canyonville, Jacksonville, and in California—
Yreka, Trinity Centre, Shasta, Red Bluff, Tehama, Chico,
Oroville, Marysville to Sacramento.

TRAVELERS AVOID RISK of OCEAN TRAVEL

Pass through the HEART OF OREGON—the Valleys of Rogue River, Umpqua and Willamette.

FARE THROUGH, FIFTY DOLLARS,
Ticket Office at Arrigoni's Hotel, Portland.
H. W. CORBETT & Co.,

Poster for Oregon line of stagecoaches to California from Portland, OR, 1866

running routes from Oakland to San Jose. When Charley wasn't working, he could be found at the local saloon, gambling and playing poker. He also worked with and broke horses. One of those horses kicked Charley in the face and caused him to lose his eye. He wore a patch over the eye for the rest of his life and some people called him, "One-Eye Charley."

But the injury never slowed Charley down. Even after the railroads began cutting into the stagecoach business, Charley kept busy farming and lumbering. He even tried his hand at raising chickens, but he really liked horses better.

In 1879, at the age of 67, Charley Parkhurst died of cancer. It was a blow to his many friends and admirers. They arranged for Charley to have a fitting burial and sent his body to the undertaker and that was when everybody learned that Charley had kept a big secret his whole life. The undertaker announced that he had learned that Charley was actually Charlotte. He was a woman.

His friends were shocked. Nobody had ever suspected that the tough, gun-slinging horse driver was a woman. Most people didn't think a woman could possibly manage horses the way Charley did. A woman couldn't fight off robbers or cut lumber. But she did.

Friends did some research and learned that Charley was actually born Charlotte Darkey Parkhurst and was orphaned at a very young age. Young Charlotte was sent to live at an orphanage in New Hampshire and she hated it. When she was 12 years old, she cut off her hair and ran away from the orphanage. She changed her name to Charley and started dressing as a boy. She found work at a stable and learned how to care for horses. Charley had a talent for riding and driving horses. At first, she drove teams of two horses, then teams of four, and finally she mastered the difficult skill of driving a team of six. Charley never told anyone her secret and spent the rest of her life as a man.

Historians believe that Charley may have been one of the first women ever to vote in the United States. The Santa Cruz Sentinel of October 17, 1868, lists Charles Darkey Parkhurst on the official poll list for the election of 1868. That vote would make Charley one of the first women to ever cast a vote for U.S. president. The United States did not give all women the right to vote until 1920.

He's Bad Medicine

During the days of the Wild West, gunfighters went by many nicknames. You knew you were facing a dangerous man if he was known as a "leather slapper," "gun fanner," or "shootist." People also called gun fighters a "curly wolf" or just plain "bad medicine."

STAGECOACH MARY

Mary Fields, c. 1895

Mary Fields needed a job. She'd just been fired from her job at the convent because of a little mistake with a gun and her coworker. She didn't hurt him very badly. And the way Mary figured it, he deserved the hole in his rear end. But it still left Mary without a job or money. So when she saw an advertisement for someone to drive the mail stagecoach, she applied.

The postmaster said he'd hire the applicant who was the fastest at hitching up a team of six horses to the coach. Mary could do that with her eyes closed and one hand tied behind her back; of course she was hired. In 1859, at the age of 60, Mary became the second woman and the first African American woman in history to work for the U.S. Postal Service.

Mary was born a slave in Hickman County, TN, around 1832. She was never sure of her birthday or age because there were no accurate records of her birth, but she spent the first 30 years of her life working the fields of Tennessee. Mary grew up to be a large woman with broad shoulders and a powerful punch. At 6 feet tall and weighing more than 200 pounds, she was as big as most men and just as tough. She was known to punch out any man she disagreed with and according to the *Great Falls Examiner* newspaper, she later broke more noses than any other person in central Montana.

She liked cigars, whiskey, and guns, and used them all. She fearlessly guarded her mail route and was always punctual. Folks in Montana said she was more reliable than the stagecoach schedule and began calling her Stagecoach Mary.

Riding her trusty mule, Moses, she rode through blizzards, thunderstorms, and blasting heat to deliver her letters and packages. If the snow was too deep for Moses to walk, she put on her snowshoes and headed out with the heavy pack on her shoulders.

Mary kept delivering mail until she was 70 years old. Then she retired to the "easier" job of running her own laundry. She washed, ironed, and starched shirts in the days before there were any washing machines and the irons had to be heated on the stove. It was a tough job and sometimes she would need to have a little fun after work, hanging out in the local saloon and drinking whiskey, smoking cigars, and spitting tobacco.

One day, she walked out of the saloon and met one of her laundry customers who had not paid his bill. Mary slugged the man in the face and knocked him out cold. She was 72 years old at the time. Needless to say, people paid their bills after that.

The people of Cascade, MT, loved Stagecoach Mary, and every year on her birthday the town closed its schools to celebrate. When the state of Montana passed a law forbidding women from entering saloons, the mayor of Cascade granted Mary an exemption.

Mary died in 1914. People reckon she was about 82 years old, give or take a couple of years.

BULLDOGGIN' BILL

THE NORMAN FILM MFG. CO.

BILL PICKETT
WORLD'S COLORED CHAMPION
'THE BULL-DOGGER'
Featuring The Colored Hero of the Mexican Bull Ring
in Death-Defying Feats of Courage and Skill
THRILLS! LAUGHS TOO!
Produced by NORMAN FILM MFG. CO.
JACKSONVILLE, FLA.

Bill sat quietly and watched the small brown bulldog chase after the cattle. When one of the steers got away from her, the bulldog would run up to the steer and bite its lip. With the bulldog pulling on its lip, the steer became cooperative and went wherever the bulldog pulled him. Bill thought about it and wondered if that would work for him. Could he wrestle a cow down and make it behave by biting it on the lip? It was worth a try. Well, at least Bill thought so.

Bill was born in Texas in 1870, the child of a former slave. Bill had 12 brothers and sisters and they all worked on the family farm. Bill's younger brother claimed that was where Bill started practicing his unusual skill of biting steers on the lip. He would ride his horse up next to the steer, jump off of his horse, and grab the steer by the horns. Then Bill would bite the lip of the steer just like he had seen the bulldogs do. The steer would completely submit when Bill was chomping on its lip.

Bill began demonstrating this technique when he was just a teenager. Audiences loved watching Bill grab the steer by the horns and bite its lip. They were amazed to see the huge horned animal roll on its side like a helpless kitten.

Soon Bill Pickett became known as Bulldoggin' Bill. He demonstrated his bulldogging technique in rodeos, circuses, and Wild West shows around the world. Other cowboys wanted to try out this new sport, but they didn't want to bite the steer on the lip. Most of them thought that part was pretty disgusting. So the sport was modified.

The rodeo would place a 500-pound steer in a chute and release it into the arena. The contestant would ride up to the animal, grab it by its horns, plant his feet on the ground, and wrestle it to the ground. A fast cowboy could wrestle the bull to the ground in 5–8 seconds.

For more than 40 years, Bill entertained people by riding wild broncos and bulls and wrestling steers. He worked for the 101 Ranch's Wild West Show for 25 years and even appeared in two cowboy movies, *The Bull-Dogger* and *The Crimson Skull*. He was the first African American cowboy to star in a film.

In 1971, he was inducted into the Cowboy Hall of Fame, and in 1994, the U.S. Postal Service issued a stamp with his picture on it.

Bill Pickett left this life just the way he spent most of it. He was working with a horse and had an accident. He died at the age of 61.

At the Cowboy Hall of Fame, these words are inscribed to Bill Pickett's memory:

Like many men in the old time West
On any job he did his best
He left a blank that's hard to fill
For there will never be another Bill.

GOODNIGHT-LOVING TRAIL

Charles Goodnight

Oliver Loving

The Civil War was over and Charles Goodnight was ready to return home to Texas and his cattle ranch. There was just one problem: The cattle were missing. Not just Goodnight's cattle. All of the ranchers in Texas had cattle that had left the ranch.

Before the start of the Civil War, Texas had been a free-range area, where cattle could roam and graze wherever they wanted. The owners branded the cattle to tell which ones were theirs and then rounded up their cattle when they were ready to take them to market. But during the Civil War, there had been no roundups. The cattle had continued to roam the hills and plains of Texas breeding and producing more calves.

At the end of the war, the Texas ranchers joined in what was called "making the gather." This meant the ranchers across the state gathered in the free-range cattle and divided them up. The herds had multiplied and there was an abundance of cattle for every rancher. It should have been good news. But there were far more cattle in Texas than there were hungry Texans. The price of beef in Texas was at an all-time low. What was a poor cowboy to do?

Goodnight met up with an older rancher, named Oliver Loving and they decided the best thing to do was to sell their cattle where there was a demand for beef. The miners, settlers, and soldiers in Colorado and New Mexico had money and they wanted beef. The only thing stopping them was hundreds of miles of dry, desert-like land, a few hundred rattlesnakes, and Native Americans who didn't like cattle ranchers.

The two cattlemen decided it was worth the risk. Other ranchers thought they were crazy. Getting the cattle from Texas to Colorado meant going through a vast waterless stretch of West Texas. Most of the other ranchers decided to take the much longer route north to Abilene, KS. It would take more time, but they knew there was water. Goodnight and Loving were willing to take the risk and set out to blaze a trail west. They herded 2,000 head of cattle from Belknap, TX, to Fort Sumner, NM. After selling some of the cattle in New Mexico, they headed on to Colorado and sold the rest. Together, they made $12,000. The average worker earned about $186 per year. They had hit the cattle jackpot.

They headed back to Texas and rounded up a couple thousand more cattle and headed out again. This time their luck didn't hold. The Native Americans who had threatened them before attacked Oliver Loving. Goodnight left the cattle in the hands of his hired cowboys and tried to nurse Loving back to health, but he died within a few days. Goodnight personally escorted his friend's body back to Texas so that Loving could be buried at his beloved home.

The death of Loving didn't stop Goodnight and other ranchers from using the trail. For nearly a decade, cattle moved north from Texas through New Mexico and on to Colorado. The trail became known as the Goodnight-Loving Trail and can still be seen today.

Goodnight built a cattle empire in Texas and even tried crossbreeding buffalo with cattle. He called them cattalo. The cattalo never did catch on with the other ranchers but his trail goes down in history as a total success.

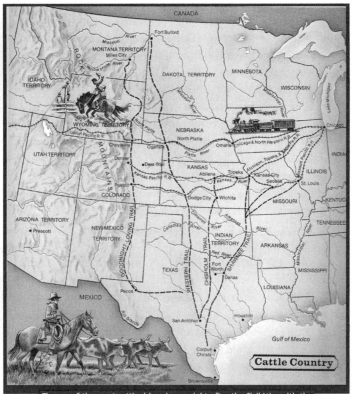

The era of the great cattle drives began right after the Civil War with the Goodnight-Loving Trail from San Angelo, TX, to Cheyene, WY, in 1866

COWPOKE PRACTICE

Cowboy in Training

One thing every cowboy and cowgirl needed to know was how to use a rope. A rope was used to capture stray animals, lead young calves, and pull animals out of the mud. It took skill and practice to learn how to throw a rope. You can make your own lasso and practice roping like a veteran cowhand.

Materials
- 6 feet of rope (cotton clothesline rope works well for this)
- Electrical tape
- Computer with Internet access
- Broomstick or small pole
- Outdoor space

Tape the ends of your rope with electrical tape so they will not fray. Then follow the steps on the instructional video below. This will show you how to tie a Honda Knot to make a lasso.

https://www.youtube.com/watch?v=4G2fzRshi18

Once you have made your rope, you can practice lassoing outside. Have an adult help place the broomstick into the ground. This will be your target. Practice swinging the rope and throwing it until you can "catch" the broomstick. As you improve, move your target farther away. (Remember this is not to be used on any people or animals. Leave that roping to the real cowboys!)

COWPOKE PRACTICE
Wild West Games

Boys and girls who lived in the Wild West liked to play games just like the children of today. They didn't have many toys that were manufactured and often had to use things they could find to play games. One of those games was called Toe Toss. It's a simple game and all you need is a few sticks from the backyard, a piece of chalk, and some friends

You will need to be barefoot for this game.

Make a mark on the ground with your chalk. This is the line that every player will stand on. Each player will take a turn standing on one foot on the line. Use the other foot to balance the stick on your toes. You have two ways to score a point. One for tossing it high. Another for getting the stick to land on the chalk mark.

73

Toss the stick with your foot and have the other players watch.

If the stick flies as high as your head, you get one point. If it lands on the chalk mark, you get a point. There is some strategy in the game because you can decide how you want to try to earn your points. Each turn you have the possibility of earning two points.

Each player will take three turns and the player with the most points at the end wins.

PISTOL PETE
★ ★ ★
THE ORIGINAL

It was the most horrible night of Frank Eaton's life. Eight-year-old Frank and his family were enjoying a quiet evening at their Kansas homestead when they heard a group of horses ride up to the cabin. They were used to travelers because their home was close to the Santa Fe Trail, but in the days after the Civil War, not all travelers were friendly.

The men called for Frank's dad. His father went to the door and stepped outside, asking what the men wanted. Gunfire rang out, and in seconds Frank's father lay dead, shot to death by a gang of Confederate Regulators. Frank's father had been a Union man and in those days, that was enough to get a man killed.

Neighbors helped Frank and his widowed mother with the farm work. They helped them survive the harsh cold winter and burning summer. One of those neighbors was a close friend of his father, Mose Beaman, and he took a special interest in Frank, teaching him the things he would have learned from his father.

One day, Beaman pulled Frank aside and said, "My boy, may an old man's curse rest upon you if you do not try to avenge your father." That day Frank told Beaman that he would hunt down the men who killed his father and get revenge. Beaman gave the boy a revolver and taught him how to mold bullets and load a cap-and-ball gun. He also taught him how to shoot.

Frank was born with a crossed left eye. This made it difficult to aim correctly, but Frank was determined. He practiced until he could hit a target without needing to sight down the barrel of a gun. He also learned to shoot with both hands.

By the time he was 15, Frank was an expert marksman. Friends claimed Frank could shoot the head off a rattlesnake with either hand. Frank left home and rode to Fort Gibson. His goal was to learn how to become a better shot from the cavalry men stationed there.

The men taught Frank how to handle a rifle, but they couldn't teach him anything about handling a pistol. Frank was better than any of the soldiers. They held a shooting competition, and Frank outshot all of the soldiers and the commanding officers.

That day, Frank was given a nickname that would stick with him for the rest of his life. Colonel Copinger awarded Frank with a marksmanship badge and told everybody that from now on they were to call Frank "Pistol Pete."

Pistol Pete's reputation for being an excellent marksman earned him a job as a deputy U.S. Marshal when he was just 17 years old. Pistol Pete was one of the youngest deputy marshal's and his territory ranged from Southern Kansas to Northern Texas.

While he was working, he always listened for clues as to where the men were who had shot his father. All of the men were known criminals, and Frank managed to track five of the six men down. Unfortunately for the men, they tried to shoot it out with Pistol Pete. They couldn't draw as fast as he did. Pete killed five of the men who had attacked his father. The sixth man was killed over a card game.

During his career as a lawman, Pistol Pete always kept a pair of loaded .45 Colts strapped to his hips, and was known to tell people that he'd rather have a pocket full of rocks than an empty gun.

Pistol Pete fell in love with a girl named Jenny. Worried about her boyfriend, Jenny gave Pistol Pete a steel cross to wear around his neck. That cross actually save Pistol Pete's life. When he got into a gunfight with some outlaws he was trying to arrest, a bullet hit him in the chest, but instead of killing him, the bullet hit the metal cross and was deflected. Pistol Pete was sure the cross saved his life.

He then started telling everybody that when he was in a fight he'd prefer to have the prayers of a good woman rather than half a dozen hot guns. Because as Pete said, "She's talking to headquarters."

Pete never got to thank Jenny for the cross that saved his life. She died of pneumonia. Pistol Pete buried the cross at the head of her grave.

Pistol Pete served many years as a deputy marshal and was involved in several gunfights. Most of the battles were with cattle rustlers and robbers who refused to surrender for

arrest. Pete was known to have 15 notches on the handle of his six-shooters: One notch for each man he had killed in a shootout.

As the West became civilized and towns sprang up in Oklahoma Territory, Pistol Pete settled down and opened a blacksmith's shop in Perkins, OK. He married and raised 10 children. Pistol Pete continued to carry his loaded pistols until the end of his life. He also wore his cowboy clothes around town. He was easy to recognize with his tall cowboy hat, jeans tucked into his boots, and two long braids of hair.

Pistol Pete on his front porch, c. 1954

As he got older, Pistol Pete enjoyed entertaining people with stories of his life in the West. He would happily demonstrate his fast-draw techniques and his shooting accuracy by shooting off the heads of matches from a distance of 20 feet. He liked to ride in parades and shoot his guns for cheering crowds.

In 1923, Pistol Pete was riding his horse in an Armistice Day parade in Stillwater, OK, when a group of students from Oklahoma State University (OSU) saw him and decided that Pistol Pete would be the perfect mascot for their school.

These days, Pistol Pete is immortalized as the OSU mascot and is the only mascot in the nation that is based on a single historical individual. OSU students believe that Pistol Pete embodies the true spirit of a cowboy in that he is loyal, doesn't back down, and always shoots straight.

Pistol Pete lived to be 97 years old and died in Oklahoma in 1958. His image is still seen today at every OSU sporting event.

Wild Bill's Last Shootout

Famous Sheriff Wild Bill Hickok was fired from his job as sheriff of Abilene, KS. He was involved in a shootout and accidentally killed his deputy, Mike Williams. Hickok said that event haunted him for the rest of his life and he never fought in another gun battle.

BELLE STARR, BANDIT QUEEN

Belle Starr, Fort Smith, AR, 1886

She wore velvet skirts with polished dainty boots and six-shooters strapped to her waist. She was Belle Starr, and she was known as the Bandit Queen.

Belle didn't start out life as a robber and thief, although her mother *was* Eliza Hatfield, related to the family in the Hatfield and McCoy feud. Belle was born Myra Maybelle Shirley and grew up in a wealthy family. Her father owned a hotel in Carthage, MO, and Belle attended the Carthage Female Academy where she learned to play the piano, speak foreign languages, and act like a lady. These lessons didn't seem to stick with Belle.

As a girl, she enjoyed riding her horse with her brother and learned how to shoot better than most of the boys. She loved to read, but she also liked to fight and, thanks to training from her brother, she was good at both.

The Civil War was hard on the town of Carthage. Bloody wars between the Missouri Confederates and the Union soldiers wrecked the town. Belle's adored brother, Bud, was killed in a raid by Union soldiers. Belle and her family were devastated. With the town in ruins, the whole family packed up and moved to Texas.

It was in Texas that Belle began her days as the Bandit Queen. While living on a farm south of Dallas, some of Bud's old friends came to visit Belle and her family. They included members of the James-Younger gang including Frank and Jesse James and the Younger brothers. The gang members hid out at Belle's home after one of their bank robberies. Belle fell in love with one of the men associated with the gang, Jim Reed, an old friend from Missouri. At that time, Reed was not yet on the Most Wanted posters, so Belle's parents agreed to the marriage.

For a time the couple was happy. Belle had a daughter named Rosie Lee who she adored and said was a beautiful pearl. The nickname stuck and she was known as Pearl Reed. After a few years of family life, however, Jim Reed wanted more adventure and more money. He began making counterfeit money and started stealing horses. This all eventually ended

Jesse and Frank James, 1872

with Reed getting shot and killed by a deputy.

After he died, Belle remarried another criminal named Sam Starr. The couple settled in an area of the West that was considered "Indian Territory," a place where it was difficult for lawmen to track criminals. Many outlaws hid in the area, and Belle was quite willing to hide them all.

COWBOY POET

Black Bart was a California bandit who had the heart of an artist. He liked writing poetry. After a successful hold-up, Black Bart would leave one of his poems in the empty safe or strongbox in hopes of confusing the posse who was hunting for him. Black Bart, whose real name was Charles E. Boles, also tried to fool the lawmen by wearing socks over his boots so he wouldn't leave any tracks.

Many historians believe that Belle was actually the brains behind all of her husbands' criminal activities. She liked to be in on the planning of any robberies and was known to be a bright, well-educated woman. She wasn't always involved in the actual robberies, although it is believed that she did hold up one stagecoach when she was dressed as a man.

But the crime that sent Belle to jail was horse theft. She was given a 6-month jail sentence that she served without a single problem. But as soon as she was released, Belle went back to her bandit ways—plotting and planning cattle rustling, horse thefts, and robberies.

Belle managed to stay alive longer than several of her outlaw friends, but on February 3, 1889, Belle Starr was found dead on a country road. She had been shot to death while riding her horse. There was an investigation into her death, but the killer was never captured.

To this day nobody knows for sure who killed the Bandit Queen. The lawmen questioned everyone involved with Belle, including her children and husband, but no one was ever arrested or tried.

After she died, publisher Richard K. Knox wrote a book that greatly exaggerated Belle's life and her crimes, *Belle Starr, The Bandit Queen or The Female Jesse James. A Full And Authentic History of the Dashing Female Highwayman*. It was a sensation and because of it, the legend of Belle Starr was born.

QUEEN ANN

Ann Bassett, also known as Queen Ann, in her younger years

Stealing cattle was her game and Ann Bassett was her name.

Ann Bassett grew up on a Colorado ranch, and by the time she was 15, she could ride, rope, and shoot as well as any of her father's ranch hands. The pretty teenager was small in stature, but known to have fiery temper. And the one thing that made Ann truly angry were the cattle barons who wanted to take over her family ranch.

The cattle barons ran thousands of head of cattle on the open-range land by Ann's family ranch. The area was called The Park and it was on land near the borders of Wyoming, CO, and Utah. In order to get Ann's family to sell their ranch, the barons tried some pretty dirty tricks including stealing or rustling some of the Bassetts' cattle.

Ann, her mother, and her sister, Josie, came up with their own solution. They stole the baron's cattle and sold as many of them as they could. Sometimes they didn't even bother to try to make a profit with their rustling. The women just wanted to get back at the barons, so they located the baron's cattle and then deliberately ran the cows over the cliffs—literally killing the baron's profits. Ann began taking the lead in planning the cattle rustling. The neighboring ranchers supported Ann in the fight against the cattle barons and started calling her Queen Ann of the cattle rustlers.

Pretty soon, the cattle barons were tired of losing their profits to Queen Ann. They hired professional gunslinger Tom Horn to "get rid" of the problem. Horn disguised himself as a regular cowboy and began investigating. Horn shot and killed two of the area ranchers who assisted in the rustling, but he left the Bassett women alone.

It may have been because Horn was warned to keep clear of Ann Bassett by her boyfriend, Butch Cassidy. The outlaws of the Wild Bunch liked to hide out in the hills and valleys near Ann's family ranch. Both Ann and Josie dated members of the gang. And received help in their cattle stealing from Butch and the Sundance Kid.

The cattle barons were determined to shut Ann down and hired a detective from the Pinkerton Agency to investigate the cattle thefts. When the detective found freshly butchered meat in a storeroom on Ann's ranch, she was arrested and charged with cattle rustling.

On the day of her trial, the courtroom was packed with people curious to see the lovely cattle rustler in person. The regular folks were cheering for the young ranch woman who had dared to stand up to the big business cattle barons. They were thrilled when the jury cleared Ann of all charges. Ann and her supporters paraded triumphantly through town.

Later in life, Ann married and moved to a small town in Utah. She lived a peaceful life until her death in 1956 at the age of 78.

THE REAL LONE RANGER
BASS REEVES

The first African-American U.S. Deputy Marshal

From 1933 to 1957, every kid in America knew the Lone Ranger. He was a Wild West hero who rode a silver horse and gave out silver coins. He fought outlaws with the help of his Native American friend, Tonto. And he was always in disguise, usually wearing a black mask. The beloved cultural icon was on radio and television for more than 20 years, but nobody ever knew that the inspiration for the Lone Ranger came from a real lawman named Bass Reeves. And they certainly never realized that the real Lone Ranger was not a White man, but a Black man who was born a slave.

During the Civil War, Bass Reeves was assigned to look after his master, George Reeves. During that time, they had an altercation. Some believe the fight was over a card game where Bass had much better cards and that made his master

angry. It ended up in a fistfight, with Bass getting the better of his master. He knew then that he had to leave because the punishment for such an offence would have been severe.

Bass ran away and ended up in Oklahoma Territory, where he lived with the Seminole Indians. A tall man at 6'2", Bass looked majestic riding his horse. He was respected by the Native Americans and became an expert marksman and rider. He got so good at shooting that he was actually banned from competing in local shooting contests. It wasn't fair for Bass to win the prize every time.

When the Emancipation Proclamation was signed, Bass was officially a free man and no longer a fugitive. He moved to Van Buren, AR, and bought a farm. He also married his sweetheart Nellie Jennie and they started a family. For the next 12 years, Bass was content as a successful farmer and father. He and Nellie had 10 children—five girls and five boys. But in 1875, District Marshal James F. Fagan came knocking at Bass Reeves' door. Oklahoma Territory had become a hideout for outlaws. Robbers and murderers were headed into Indian Territory to hide out from the law. Fagan wanted to hire Bass to serve a U.S. Marshal.

Bass agreed to serve. Because he spoke several Native American languages, Bass often hired Seminole and Creek Indians as assistants. He couldn't read or write, but that didn't hinder his effectiveness. Bass would have somebody read the arrest warrants to him and with his impeccable memory, he knew exactly who he was tracking and why. He never made a mistake with his warrants.

A master of disguises, Bass would dress up as a cowboy or a farmer. Sometimes he pretended to be an outlaw himself. When he was trailing some outlaws in Red River Valley, TX, he put on dirty, worn-out clothes and hid his handcuffs, pistol, and badge under his clothes. He then "wandered" for several miles, acting like a tramp scrounging for food. In reality, he knew exactly where he was going, but he wanted to make sure if that anyone was watching, then he or she would be convinced of his story.

Bass reached the farmhouse where he suspected the robbers were hiding out and asked the woman of the house for some food. He told her a sad story of how he had been chased by a posse just for stealing a bit of money.

The woman felt sorry for Bass and suggested that he should meet her sons. That was exactly what Bass was hoping for. By suppertime, Bass and the young outlaws were exchanging stories about their crimes and how they were hiding from the law. Bass agreed to spend the night and show the two outlaws a good escape route in the morning.

When the outlaws were asleep, Bass handcuffed them. In the morning, he woke them up and marched them at gunpoint to his camp. Their mother ran after him screaming that he had pulled a dirty trick. A few days later, Bass turned the men in to the state and received his reward.

Bass served as a U.S. Marshal for 35 years. He brought in more than 3,000 outlaws and helped to make Oklahoma Territory a safer place.

He said he "never shot a man when it was not necessary for him to do so in the discharge of his duty to save his own life." Bass often gave out silver coins to the people who worked with him. He usually rode a white horse and he often had Native Americans helping him. These are very similar to the traits of the television icon Lone Ranger. That is why most people believe that Bass Reeves was the true inspiration for the Lone Ranger.

BAT MASTERSON

    The streets of Dodge City were full of noise. Rowdy cowboys were in town getting drunk and starting fights. Music from the dance halls spilled out into the streets and so did their patrons, all smelling of whiskey and sweat. It was a typical night in Dodge and a team of lawmen was patrolling the streets watching for trouble.

    The use of firearms was forbidden in the city limits, and cowboys were supposed to check their guns with the bartender at the saloon. It was one way the sheriff and his men could help reduce the number of men killed over a card game gone wrong. But there was always somebody who disobeyed the rules and argued about turning over their gun. That night deputy Ed Masterson ran into two drunken cowboys who refused to give up their weapons.

Ed and his brother Bat Masterson had been part of Wyatt Earp's clean-up crew, charged with taming the wildest city in the West. The team of cowboys had been selected by Earp because of their calm temperaments and their skill with a gun. Bat was an especially excellent marksman. In just a few months, the sheriff and his deputies had drastically reduced the crime

Bat Masterson, 1879

and murders in Dodge City. But there was more work to do.

Wyatt Earp and Bat were patrolling another street in town when the cowboys stumbled out of the saloon. Ed, however, saw the cowboys *and* their guns. He knew drunken men and firearms were not a good combination. He told the cowboys to hand over their weapons, but they refused. Ed had no choice; he had to try to take the guns from the cowboys. A friend of Ed's stepped in to help but one of the cowboys aimed the pistol in his face and fired. Fortunately the gun misfired. Ed was even more determined to take the guns away. He was afraid innocent bystanders could get killed.

As Ed reached for the gun, the other cowboy shot Ed in the abdomen. Ed stumbled away. The blast from the gunshot was so close it caused his shirt and coat to catch on fire. By this time, Bat was just a few feet away from the fight. He pulled his gun and quickly shot the two cowboys. Then he rushed to help his brother. Ed died in Bat's arms. It was a tragedy that Bat would never forget.

The cowboy who shot Ed died from the gunshot wound inflicted by Bat. The other cowboy lived and was allowed to return to Texas without being charged. Bat continued his work as a lawman and as a scout for the military. As his arrest numbers grew, so did his reputation. He achieved more fame when he captured "Dirty Dave" Rudabaugh, a noted killer, cattle rustler, and gunfighter.

Bat liked life in the West, but he also liked the finer things in life that could be found in the East. He liked nice clothes and usually dressed in a suit with a derby hat perched on his head. He sometimes used a finely carved cane because of an old injury from one of his first shootouts. Bat also liked sports of all kinds. He followed baseball and promoted boxing matches.

In 1902, Bat and his wife, Emma, moved to New York City. The world of tall buildings and busy streets was totally different from the dusty trails and buffalo hunts of Bat's younger years. But Bat was starting a new career. At the age of 49, he began work as a sports reporter.

Bat became a popular figure in New York and before long, he was writing a regular column about sports, entertainment, and politics for the *New York Morning Telegraph*. The old cowboy continued writing newspaper stories and entertaining people with tales of his life in the West until his death in 1921.

He died of a heart attack while he was sitting at his desk at the *Telegraph* newspaper office. He had just finished writing his morning column. He was 67 years old.

THE MYSTERY OF BUTCH CASSIDY

Front row left to right: Harry A. Longabaugh, alias the Sundance Kid; Ben Kilpatrick, alias the Tall Texan; Robert Leroy Parker, alias Butch Cassidy. Standing: Will Carver, alias News Carver; Harvey Logan, alias Kid Curry. Fort Worth, TX, 1900

Butch Cassidy had it all: brains, good looks, and charm. And he used all of these talents to pull off some of the biggest bank and train robberies in the history of the West. Butch Cassidy was considered the leader of the Wild Bunch, a gang of horse thieves and robbers that included Harry Longabaugh, also known as the Sundance Kid. In 5 short years, they managed to steal the modern-day equivalent of $10 million dollars.

Cassidy himself was not in favor of personal violence and claimed he had never killed a man. In shootouts, he claimed he aimed for the horses. But he was definitely in favor of dynamite and used it to blow open trains and safes to steal the contents.

One of the Wild Bunch's most famous robberies was the Wilcox Train Robbery of 1899. The train was traveling through Wyoming headed for the town of Medicine Bow. It had been raining all night and the engineer was watching for signals that bridges might be washed out. At 2:18 in the morning, the engineer saw a signalman waving him down. The engineer slowed the train to a stop and sent out one of the crew to get the report. If the bridge was washed out, it would mean a very long delay in delivery of passengers and goods.

The engineer was shocked when two men with guns boarded the engine. Their faces were covered with cloths and they demanded all of the money and gold the train was carrying. If the crew didn't give it to them, then the bandits said they had enough dynamite to blow open the safes.

The crew and passengers were marched off the train at gunpoint. The robbers took hatpins, watches, and cuff links,

Why Is He the Sundance Kid?

Harry Longabaugh got his nickname, the Sundance Kid, because he served a jail term for stealing a horse in Sundance, WY.

then they set to work on opening the safe. It took just a few sticks of dynamite to explode the train car and the safe. The robbers grabbed unsigned bank notes, cash, and gold that totaled more than $30,000. (In today's money, that's more than $800,000!)

The robbers were never caught, but all of the detectives and railroad investigators were sure it was the work of Butch Cassidy and his Wild Bunch. During the next 3 years, Butch Cassidy masterminded so many successful train robberies that the railroad investigators gave up trying to catch him. Instead they said that if Cassidy would turn himself in, then they would give him amnesty. No charges would be filed against him and they would hire him as a guard with a good paycheck. Cassidy turned them down.

Frustrated, the railroads hired the famous Pinkerton National Detective Agency to hunt down Butch and his fellow outlaws. The Pinkerton men stayed right on Cassidy's tail and made it difficult for him to continue his thieving in the United States. In 1901, Cassidy left the United States for South America. He traveled with his friends, the Sundance Kid and his girlfriend, Etta Place.

Once he was in South America, Cassidy seemed to settle down. He purchased a 15,000-acre ranch in Argentina and began raising cattle. But strangely in 1908, Cassidy and Longabaugh seemed to take up the life of crime. On November 3, a Bolivian courier carrying a payroll was attacked and robbed by two masked American bandits. The bandits hid out in a small mining town of San Vicente. The owner of their lodging house noticed the mule they had with them had the brand of the Aramayo mine. He contacted the Bolivian army about his suspicious boarders, and three soldiers were sent to investigate.

Hanging Judge

Judge Isaac Parker was known as the hanging judge because during his reign as judge in Fort Smith, AR, he sentenced 156 men and four women to the hangman's noose. But most of the hangings were never carried out. None of the women were ever actually sent to the gallows and just 76 men were hanged by Judge Parker.

On the night of November 6, the boardinghouse was surrounded by the three soldiers, the police chief, the mayor, and some other city officials. When the soldiers approached the house, the bandits inside opened fire. They shot and killed one officer and wounded another. Immediately there was a vicious gunfight.

At 2 a.m., there was a pause in the fighting and the officials heard a man screaming inside the house. Then they heard a gunshot. A few seconds later, there was another gunshot. Then there was total silence.

It wasn't until the light of the next morning that the officials entered the house. There they found two dead bodies. They were filled with bullet holes and each one had a gunshot to the head. The local police believed that one bandit probably shot his fatally wounded partner in the head and then killed himself.

The reports of their deaths made headlines in America. But people could not believe that two famous outlaws had killed themselves in a foreign country. Why had they given up in Bolivia when they had been in tougher situations in America?

The Bolivian police had no idea that Cassidy and Longabaugh were so famous in the United States, so they never took pictures of the dead bandits. They simply buried the bodies.

Rumors started to flow that Butch Cassidy and the Sundance Kid had staged their deaths and had actually escaped to Europe or were starting new lives in America. It was even rumored that Butch Cassidy had gotten plastic surgery in Europe so he could return to live a quiet life in America.

Speculation about the two outlaws has gone on for a century. In 2002, NOVA filmed a special documentary about their lives and even tried to dig up their bodies in Bolivia so they could do DNA testing. The DNA results were inconclusive. The tests neither confirmed nor denied that the bodies were Butch and Sundance. Researchers are still trying to prove that the famous duo died that day in Bolivia.

THE STRANGE CASE OF ETTA PLACE

It's a mystery that has stumped historians for more than 100 years. Who was Etta Place and where did she go?

Etta was known to be the longtime girlfriend of the Sundance Kid (Harry Longabaugh). A detective from the Pinkerton agency described her as having "classic good looks" and being about 5'4" to 5'5" in height and between 110 and 115 pounds. And the Pinkerton detectives should know—they spent several years following her. But they never caught her and they never figured out where she went or where she came from in the first place.

Nobody knows for sure where Etta Place was born, or if Etta Place is even her real name. The first time Etta was introduced as Sundance's girlfriend was sometime in 1900. Rumor was that she was a young schoolteacher who had left her family and run off to be with the robber, but there is no hard evidence to back that up. Another rumor was that she was a woman from a brothel, but again there is no evidence.

What the Pinkerton Detectives did know was that in 1901, Etta traveled to New York City with Sundance and posed for a picture at a photographic studio.

From there, she traveled with both Butch and Sundance to Buenos Aires. She lived with the two outlaws on a ranch they bought in Argentina. There they set up a cattle ranch and seemed to be settled for a few years. She made at least two trips back to the United States and even attended the 1904 World's Fair in St. Louis—the whole time being watched by the Pinkerton men.

Harry Longabaugh (the Sundance Kid) and Etta Place, just before they sailed for South America

Then in 1906, Etta sailed back to San Francisco with Sundance. She stayed in California, and Sundance went back to South America. Just a few months later, both Butch and Sundance were killed in a shootout after a robbery in Bolivia. At least, that's the official story.

Strangely, soon after the deaths of Butch and Sundance, Etta Place disappeared—never to be heard of or seen again. Did she change her name and move to another part of the United States? That is one possibility.

The facts are that the last known address for Etta Place was San Francisco in 1907. In 1909, a woman who matched Etta's description requested a death certificate from Bolivia for the Sundance Kid. The woman claimed she needed it to settle his estate, but she never received a certificate. That is the last time she is recorded in history.

Some people speculate that Etta Place and Ann Bassett were actually the same person. Their pictures do look similar, as you can see here.

Etta Place   Ann Bassett

And one researcher even had the photographs of their faces analyzed. The researcher's conclusion was that they were the same person. The theory is that Etta was Ann Bassett's alias. But, at the time Etta was supposed to be in South America with Sundance and Butch, Ann Bassett was in jail for cattle rustling. It would be impossible for Ann Bassett to be in two places at once.

 ## Cole Younger, Retired Outlaw

Not all outlaws died in a blaze of gunfire. Cole Younger was a member of the Younger-James Gang and robbed banks and trains with Jesse James. But Younger was caught and sentenced to 20 years in prison. When he was released, Younger went straight. He got a job selling tombstones and lived quietly in Lee Summit, MO, where he was known to be a church-going man. He died in 1916 at the age of 72.

Other researchers speculate that she simply changed her name and went back to work as a schoolteacher. Another report says that a woman matching her description was killed in a domestic dispute in Argentina in 1922. Still, another report says she committed suicide in Argentina in 1924. None of the reports has been verified as truth. To this day, no one is sure what happened to Etta Place.

Of course, one rumor that many people like to believe is that the deaths of Butch Cassidy and the Sundance Kid were just a scam to throw the detectives off their trail. In that scenario, Sundance comes back for Etta and they disappear to live out their lives anonymously. But there is no evidence for that theory either. It's a mystery waiting to be solved.

THE SECRET OF CATHAY WILLIAMS

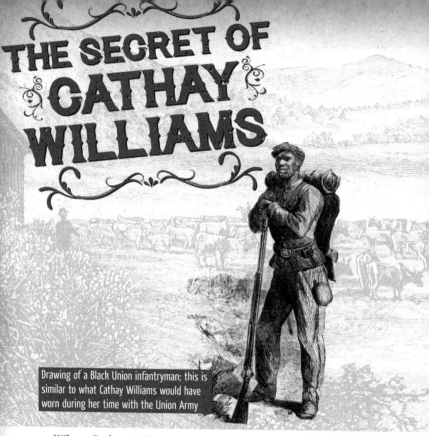

Drawing of a Black Union infantryman; this is similar to what Cathay Williams would have worn during her time with the Union Army

When Cathay Williams was born, she was automatically deemed a slave. It didn't matter that her father was a free man. All that mattered was that her mother was a slave. Any baby born to a slave stayed a slave. For the first 17 years of her life, Cathay worked as a house slave, doing laundry, cooking meals, ironing, and gardening on the Johnson plantation near Jefferson City, MO.

When the Civil War broke out, the Union soldiers took over the Johnson plantation. The slaves were all considered contraband and Cathay along with her fellow slaves were forced to go to work for the Union Army.

While today it seems a horrible fate to be forced to march with the Army and do its laundry, it was actually an improvement for Cathay. For the first time in her life, she received wages for her work. While it wasn't a great deal of money and some months there wasn't any pay at all, it was still more than she had received as a slave.

Cathay served as a cook and laundress for the 8th Indiana Voluntary Infantry Regiment and her commander was Colonel William Plummer Benton. Cathay followed the troops as they marched through the swamps of Louisiana and the mountains of Georgia. She was there for the bloody battle of Pea Ridge and the Red River Campaign. When the war ended, she was serving at Jefferson Barracks in Missouri.

Cathay knew that times were tough for people after the Civil War ended. Jobs were scarce and she wanted to keep earning money. She had spent 4 years following the military. She'd seen bodies ripped apart by mortars; she had been in the middle of gunfire and battles. She knew she could survive in the Army, but the problem was, they wouldn't let a woman enlist.

Cathay decided her best opportunity was to lie. She only told one friend and her cousin, both in the Army, of her plan to pretend she was a man and enlist too.

At 5'9" Cathay was tall for a woman. With her hair cut off and no real physical examination, she was able to get past the Army medical tests. A recruiting officer described her as 5'9", with black eyes, black hair, and black complexion. Cathay just switched her names around and enlisted as William Cathay. She told the recruiting officer she was a cook.

The next few months were ones of hard physical challenges. Her unit of Black soldiers was sent from the St. Louis area to Ft. Riley, KS. There they helped defend ranchers and settlers from attacks from angry Native Americans. The Indian tribes were angry because settlers had taken their land. Cathay and her unit escorted and guarded settlers, ranchers, and railroad crews as they worked in the West. From Ft. Riley, Cathay marched with the Buffalo Soldiers west to Fort Bayar, NM. Cathay marched hundreds of miles on foot and most of the time she was in severe pain. She was examined by army doctors and admitted to the Army hospital, but it is questionable how good the medical care was because the doctors never figured out that William Cathay was actually a woman.

In 1868, after 2 years of service, Cathay was hospitalized again for pain in her feet. This time she was diagnosed with neuralgia, probably as a result of diabetes. This doctor did a full examination and reported that Cathay was indeed a woman. She was immediately discharged from military service.

Suddenly without employment, Cathay went back to work as a laundress in Fort Union, NM. Eventually she moved to Colorado and settled there. It wasn't until 1876 that her secret of serving as a man in the military became known to the public. A reporter from St. Louis interviewed her and her story was published in the *St. Louis Daily Times*.

As Cathay aged, her years of marching during the Civil War and the Army had taken their toll. She eventually had to have all of her toes amputated and could only walk with the help of a crutch or cane. She applied for disability benefits from the military but was denied.

She died in 1892 at the age of 50. Today she is recognized as the first female African American soldier and the only female to ever serve with the Buffalo Soldiers.

Buffalo Soldiers by Frederick Remington, 1888

Buffalo Soldiers

Photograph of a group of African-American soldiers at Camp Wikoff, New York, c. 1898

In 1866 and 1867, Congress authorized the formation of four African American regiments in the United States Cavalry. These soldiers were assigned to work in the Indian territories. The Native Americans gave the Black units the nickname "Buffalo Soldiers." The soldiers enlisted for 5 years and received $13 a month—much better wages than they could earn in civilian life.

There are several theories as to why the Native Americans called them Buffalo Soldiers. It may have been that the curly hair of the African Americans reminded the Indians of the buffalo. Or, because the soldiers were considered fierce and brave as buffalo. Others suggest it's because of the buffalo-hide coats the soldiers wore in the winter.

COWPOKE PRACTICE
Bulls & Cows

This is a fun paper-and-pencil game that only requires two people.

The object of this game is to be the first person to guess your opponent's secret number.

Materials

- ❑ Two players
- ❑ Paper
- ❑ Pencil

Each person writes a four-digit number on a piece of paper. Don't tell what the number is—it's a secret!

The digits must all be different. For example, you can use 5821 but not 5835. Pick one person to go first. (You will switch on the next round.)

One player, the chooser, thinks of a four-digit number and the other player, the guesser, tries to figure it out. At each turn, the guesser tries a four-digit number and the chooser says how close it is to the answer by giving:

* the number of bulls, or the digits correct in the right position, and
* the number of cows, or the digits correct but in the wrong position.

The guesser tries to guess the answer in the fewest number of turns.

If either number has repeated digits, the rule is that each digit can only count toward the score once and bulls are counted before cows.

For example, if the chooser has thought of the number 2745, the replies for some guesses are as follows:

Guess: 1389; Reply: 0 Bulls, 0 Cows
Guess: 1234; Reply: 0 Bulls, 2 Cows
Guess: 1759; Reply: 1 Bull, 1 Cow
Guess: 1785; Reply: 2 Bulls, 0 Cows
Guess: 2745; Reply: 4 Bulls

BIBLIOGRAPHY

AUTHOR'S NOTE

Dear Readers,

I hope you liked learning the truth in the Top Secret Files. I have worked hard to research each story and verify its authenticity. Sometimes there are differences of opinions between historians as to what exactly happened and when. I've used the information that is currently regarded as true. But like every good mystery, sometimes new clues will be found and this might change our view of history.

The quotes in these books are words that the historical figures used. I have tried to capture the spirit of when and how the words would have been heard; therefore, sometimes the dialogue has been embellished or re-imagined to fit the spirit of the story. As a history detective, I will continue to research and dig for clues that will tell me more about history and the people who made it. You might want to look into some of the sources I used for my research (listed below) if you are interested in learning more about this fascinating period of history.

—Stephanie Bearce

BOOKS

Brennan, S. (2005). *The greatest cowboy stories ever told.* Guilford, CT: The Lyons Press.

Cody, B. B. (1920). *An autobiography of Buffalo Bill (Colonel W. F. Cody).* Retrieved from http://www.gutenberg.org/files/12740/12740-h/12740-h.htm

Dary, D. (1996). *Seeking pleasure in the old West.* New York, NY: Alfred A Knopf.

Dary, D. (1979). *True tales of the old time plains.* New York, NY: Crown Publishers.

The gunfighters. (1981). Alexandria, VA: Time Life Books.

Rollins, P. A. (1997). *The cowboy: An unconventional history of civilization on the old-time cattle range.* Norman: University of Oklahoma Press.

Wagner, T. M. (2011). *Black cowboys of the old West: True, sensational, and little-known stories from history.* Helena, MT: TwoDot.

Walker, D. L. (1997). *Legends and lies: Great mysteries of the American West.* New York, NY: Forge Press.

WEBSITES

The autobiography of "Queen" Ann Bassett. (2014). Retrieved from http://www.amberandchaos.net/?p=21

Bates, D. (2011). Is this the face of Butch Cassidy and proof he didn't die in 1908 shootout with the Bolivian army? *Daily Mail.* Retrieved from http://www.dailymail.co.uk/news/article-2026223/Proof-Butch-Cassidy-DIDNT-die-1908-shootout-Bolivian-army.html

Biography.com. (n.d.). *Wild Bill Hickok.* Retrieved from http://www.biography.com/people/wild-bill-hickok-40262#early-years

BlackCowboys.com. (n.d.). *Famous cowboys: Mary Fields.* Retrieved from http://www.blackcowboys. com/maryfields.htm

BlackCowboys.com. (n.d.). *Famous cowboys: Nat Love.* Retrieved from http://www.blackcowboys.com/nat love.htm

The Bloody Benders: America's first serial killers. (n.d.). *Mental Floss.* Retrieved from http://mental floss.com/article/53672/bloody-benders-americas-first-serial-killers

Brand, J. (2011). *The history of the American West cattle branding.* Retrieved from http://buckarooleather. blogspot.com/2011/01/history-of-american-west-cattle.html

Bristow, K. (2008). Those daring stage drivers. *California State Parks.* Retrieved from http://www.parks.ca. gov/?page_id=25451

The Buffalo Bill Museum and Grave. (n.d.). *History and research.* Retrieved from http://www.buffalobill. org/History%20Research%20on%20the%20Buffalo %20Bill%20Museum/index.html

Buffalo Soldiers of the American West. (n.d.). *A brief history of the Buffalo Soldiers.* Retrieved from http:// www.buffalosoldiers-amwest.org/history.htm

The code of the West. (n.d.). Retrieved from http://www. jcs-group.com/oldwest/cowboy/code.html

Cowboy clothes, 1800s. (n.d.). Retrieved from http://www. american-historama.org/1881-1913-maturation-era/cowboy-clothes-1800s.htm

Cowboy Way. (n.d.). *Roy Rogers' rider's rules.* Retrieved from http://www.cowboyway.com/RoyRogers.htm

Drewry, J. M. (n.d.). *Mary Fields.* Retrieved from http:// www.cascademontana.com/mary.htm

Edison, R. (n.d.). *Chuckwagon history.* Retrieved from http://americanchuckwagoncooking.blogspot.com/p/chuckwagon-historythere-is-majestic.html

Eyewitness to History.com. (2008). *Pony Express rider, 1861.* Retrieved from http://www.eyewitnesstohistory.com/ponyexpress.htm

Famous Texans.com. (n.d.). *Bill Pickett.* Retrieved from http://www.famoustexans.com/billpickett.htm

Frank Eaton Historical Home. (2014). *The legend of Pistol Pete.* Retrieved from http://www.eatonhome.org/legend

Haeber, J. (2003). Vaqueros: The first cowboys of the open range. *National Geographic.* Retrieved from http://news.nationalgeographic.com/news/2003/08/0814_030815_cowboys_2.html

Hawkins, V. (2015). *The U.S. Army's "Camel Corps" experiment.* Retrieved from https://armyhistory.org/the-u-s-armys-camel-corps-experiment/

History.com. (n.d.). *This day in history: Buffalo Bill's Wild West Show opens.* Retrieved from http://www.history.com/this-day-in-history/buffalo-bills-wild-west-show-opens

King, G. (2013). When New York City tamed the famed gunslinger Bat Masterson. *Smithsonian Magazine.* Retrieved from http://www.smithsonianmag.com/history/when-new-york-city-tamed-the-feared-gunslinger-bat-masterson-14420527/?no-ist

Lequoia, A. (n.d.). *Cowboy etiquette: Mind yer manners!* Retrieved from https://stargazermercantile.com/cowboy-etiquette-mind-yer-manners/

Livingston, P. (2015). The history of the vaquero. *American Cowboy.* Retrieved from http://www.americancowboy.com/article/history-vaquero

Lost Dutchman Days. (2007). *Legend of the Lost Dutchman Mine.* Retrieved from http://www.lost dutchmandays.org/legend.htm

The mystery of Ann Bassett and Etta Place. (2013). *Mental Floss.* Retrieved from http://mentalfloss. com/article/51368/mystery-ann-bassett-and-etta-place

National Park Service. (n.d.). *Pony Express: History & culture.* Retrieved from http://www.nps.gov/poex/ learn/historyculture/index.htm

Nix, E. (2015). *6 things you may not know about Butch Cassidy.* Retrieved from http://www.history.com/ news/history-lists/6-things-you-might-not-know-about-butch-cassidy

Pony Express National Museum. (2015). [Timeline]. Retrieved from http://ponyexpress.org/pony-express-historical-timeline/

Raine, L. (n.d.). *Cowboy personal gear.* Retrieved from http://www.cowboyshowcase.com/personal-gear. html#.VYoHQZVRHIU

Ramos, M. G. (n.d.). Cattle drives start in earnest after the Civil War. *Texas Almanac.* Retrieved from http://texasalmanac.com/topics/agriculture/cattle-drives-started-earnest-after-civil-war

Stamp, J. (2013). Decoding the range: The secret language of cattle branding. *Smithsonian Magazine.* Retrieved from http://www.smithsonianmag.com/ arts-culture/decoding-the-range-the-secret-language-of-cattle-branding-45246620/

Study.com. (n.d.). *Buffalo soldiers: History & facts.* Retrieved from http://study.com/academy/lesson/ buffalo-soldiers-history-facts-quiz.html

Wall, H. (2013). Bass Reeves: The real Lone Ranger. *This Land.* Retrieved from http://thislandpress.com/roundups/bass-reeves-the-real-lone-ranger/

Weisbrode, K. (2012). The short life of the camel corps. *New York Times.* Retrieved from http://opinionator.blogs.nytimes.com/2012/12/27/the-short-life-of-the-camel-corps/?_r=0

Weiser, K. (2010). California legends: Rattlesnake Dick's stolen loot. *Legends of America.* Retrieved from http://www.legendsofamerica.com/ca-treasures2.html

Weiser, K. (2012). Images of the American West: Deadwood, South Dakota photo gallery. *Legends of America.* Retrieved from http://www.legendsofamerica.com/picturepages/PP-Deadwood1-1876.html

Weiser, K. (2012). Old West legends: Frank B. "Pistol Pete" Eaton—Fastest draw in Indian territory. *Legends of America.* Retrieved from http://www.legendsofamerica.com/law-frankeaton.html

Weiser, K. (2012). Old West legends: Isaac Parker—Hanging judge of Indian territory. *Legends of America.* Retrieved from http://www.legendsofamerica.com/ar-isaacparker.html

Weiser, K. (2014). Old West legends: The code of the West. *Legends of America.* Retrieved from http://www.legendsofamerica.com/we-codewest.html

Weiser, K. (2015). Arizona legends: The Lost Dutchman Mine. *Legends of America.* Retrieved from http://www.legendsofamerica.com/az-lostdutchman.html

Weiser, K. (2015). Old West legends: Bass Reeves—Black hero marshal. *Legends of America.* Retrieved from http://www.legendsofamerica.com/we-bassreeves.html

Weiser, K. (2015). Old West legends: Belle Starr—The bandit queen. *Legends of America.* Retrieved from http://www.legendsofamerica.com/we-bellestarr.html

Weiser, K. (2015). Old West legends: Nat Love, aka Deadwood Dick—The greatest Black cowboy in the West. *Legends of America.* Retrieved from http://www.legendsofamerica.com/we-natlove.html

Weiser, K. (2015). Old West legends: Old West facts and trivia. *Legends of America.* Retrieved from http://www.legendsofamerica.com/we-facts.html

The West Film Project. (2001). *William F. Cody.* Retrieved from http://www.pbs.org/weta/thewest/people/a_c/buffalobill.htm

Wikipedia. (n.d.). *Ann Bassett.* Retrieved from https://en.wikipedia.org/wiki/Ann_Bassett

Wikipedia. (n.d.). *Bat Masterson.* Retrieved from https://en.wikipedia.org/wiki/Bat_Masterson

Wikipedia. (n.d.). *Belle Starr.* Retrieved from https://en.wikipedia.org/wiki/Belle_Starr

Wikipedia. (n.d.). *Bill Pickett.* Retrieved from https://en.wikipedia.org/wiki/Bill_Pickett

Wikipedia. (n.d.). *Bloody Benders.* Retrieved from https://en.wikipedia.org/wiki/Bloody_Benders

Wikipedia. (n.d.). *Charley Parkhurst.* Retrieved from https://en.wikipedia.org/wiki/Charley_Parkhurst

Wikipedia. (n.d.). *Etta Place.* Retrieved from https://en.wikipedia.org/wiki/Etta_Place

Wikipedia. (n.d.). *Mary Fields.* Retrieved from https://en.wikipedia.org/wiki/Mary_Fields

ABOUT THE AUTHOR

Stephanie Bearce is a writer, a teacher, and a history detective. She loves tracking down spies and uncovering secret missions from the comfort of her library in St. Charles, MO. When she isn't writing or teaching, Stephanie loves to travel the world and go on adventures with her husband, Darrell.

More Books in This Series

Stealthy spies, secret weapons, and special missions are just part of the mysteries uncovered when kids dare to take a peek at the *Top Secret Files*. Featuring books that focus on often unknown aspects of history, this series is sure to hook even the most reluctant readers, taking them on a journey as they try to unlock some of the secrets of our past.

Top Secret Files: The American Revolution

George Washington had his own secret agents, hired pirates to fight the British, and helped Congress smuggle weapons, but you won't learn that in your history books! Learn the true stories of the American Revolution and how spies used musket balls, books, and laundry to send messages. Discover the female Paul Revere, solve a spy puzzle, and make your own disappearing ink. It's all part of the true stories from the *Top Secret Files: The American Revolution*.

ISBN-13: 978-1-61821-247-4

Top Secret Files: The Civil War

The Pigpen Cipher, the Devil's Coffee Mill, and germ warfare were all a part of the Civil War, but you won't learn that in your history books! Discover the truth about Widow Greenhow's spy ring, how soldiers stole a locomotive, and the identity of the mysterious "Gray Ghost." Then learn how to build a model submarine and send secret light signals to your friends. It's all part of the true stories from the *Top Secret Files: The Civil War*.

ISBN-13: 978-1-61821-250-4

Top Secret Files: The Cold War

Poison dart umbrellas and cyanide guns were all a part of the arsenal of tools used by spies of the Soviet KGB, American CIA, and British MI6, but you won't learn that in your history books! Learn the true stories of the Cold War and how spies used listening devices planted in live cats and wristwatch cameras. Discover how East Germans tried to ride zip lines to freedom, while the Cambridge Four infiltrated Britain and rockets raced to the moon. Then make your own submarines and practice writing secret codes. It's all part of the true stories from the *Top Secret Files: The Cold War*.

ISBN-13: 978-1-61821-419-5 • **Available August 2015**

Top Secret Files: Gangsters and Bootleggers

Blind pigs, speakeasies, coffin varnish, and tarantula juice were all a part of the Roaring 20s. Making alcohol illegal didn't get rid of bars and taverns or crime bosses—they just went underground. Secret joints were in almost every large city. Discover the crazy language and secret codes of the Prohibition Era—why you should mind your beeswax and watch out for the gumshoe talking to the fuzz or you might end up in the cooler! It's all part of the true stories from the *Top Secret Files: Gangsters and Bootleggers*.

ISBN-13: 978-1-61821-461-4 • **Available October 2015**

Top Secret Files: Pirates and Buried Treasure

Pirates of the Golden Age had to deal with scurvy, fight ferocious battles, and eat everything from monkeys to snakes to sea turtles, but you won't learn that in your history books! Discover the truth about Anne Bonny, the Irish woman who was a true Pirate of the Caribbean, and the secrets of Blackbeard and the daring pirate Cheng I Sao. Then learn how to talk like a pirate and make a buried treasure map for your friends. It's all part of the true stories from the *Top Secret Files: Pirates and Buried Treasure*.

ISBN-13: 978-1-61821-421-8 • **Available August 2015**

Top Secret Files: World War I

Flame throwers, spy trees, bird bombs, and Hell Fighters were all a part of World War I, but you won't learn that in your history books! Uncover long-lost secrets of spies like Howard Burnham, "The One Legged Wonder," and nurse-turned-spy, Edith Cavell. Peek into secret files to learn the truth about the Red Baron and the mysterious Mata Hari. Then learn how to build your own Zeppelin balloon and mix up some invisible ink. It's all part of the true stories from the *Top Secret Files: World War I*.

ISBN-13: 978-1-61821-241-2

Top Secret Files: World War II

Spy school, poison pens, exploding muffins, and Night Witches were all a part of World War II, but you won't learn that in your history books! Crack open secret files and read about the mysterious Ghost Army, rat bombs, and doodlebugs. Discover famous spies like the White Mouse, super-agent Garbo, and baseball player and spy, Moe Berg. Then build your own secret agent kit and create a spy code. It's all part of the true stories from the *Top Secret Files: World War II*.

ISBN-13: 978-1-61821-244-3